Bones & Blue Eyes

and other stories of life

Edited by
Claire Bell & Pete Court

ISBN 978-0-6455379-7-0

Compilation copyright © Claire Bell and Pete Court 2022
Copyright of individual chapters remains with the author of those chapters.

All rights reserved. Other than for the purposes and subject to the conditions prescribed under the Copyright Act, no part of this publication may be reproduced, stored in a retrieval system, or transmitted in any form or by any means, electronic, mechanical, photocopying, recording or otherwise, without the prior permission of the publisher.

Cataloguing-in-Publication entry is available from the National Library of Australia http:/catalogue.nla.gov.au/.

This edition first published in 2022

Typesetting by Ben Morton

Published in Australia by Immortalise via Ingram Spark
www.immortalise.com.au

Front cover photograph by Alexandru Zdrobau on UnSplash
Cover layout Ben Morton

Sponsors

We wish to thank the following organisations for their sponsorship of the Stories of Life creative writing competition and publishing venture:

Omega Writers sponsoring the 2022 Stories of Life competition.

Immortalise supporting the publication, sales and distribution of the 2022 anthology.

Tabor College of Higher Education hosting the official launch of the 2022 anthology.

Thanks also to **1079 Life** for their help with promotion and support for Stories of Life.

Introduction

About eight years ago a group of passionate storytellers gathered together around a common dream. To encourage people to share their personal stories of life. And so the *Stories of Life* competition was born. People from around Adelaide were encouraged to write their personal stories of faith and testimony. And they did, and they still do. Now, as you dive into this, the seventh annual anthology, you'll see stories from all around the world. It has grown bigger than we could have imagined. Over the seven editions of *Stories of Life* we have published more than 300 stories of personal faith and testimony.

But having a story to tell does not make one a storyteller. So the decision was made to make available everything a person might need to learn how to write their own story, to become a storyteller. All those resources are still there for you at www.storiesoflife.net, because, as we said eight years ago, these stories need to be told. Why? Because these stories are not made up, they are not just entertainment. They are all, each and every one of them, a testament to a God who is not only impossibly powerful but is also incredibly personal and present. By sharing these stories, and the stories that will grace future editions, we all become more aware that every one of us has a story. It's a story to tell, and it's a story of life.

This year is the first without the full involvement of our inaugural and guiding editor, Mark Worthing; he has, however, acted as consultant as we take up where he left off. We must give huge thanks for his drive, passion and wisdom over the years. We must also thank the vibrant folk at Omega Christian Writers, who are helping to push this wonderful concept across the nation. Like every one of God's amazing projects, *Stories of Life* is driven by individuals who are committed. The list of names is long and illustrious. But rather than thank you all here, we will use the space with more of this year's truly excellent *Stories of Life*.

Enjoy.

Pete Court
Convenor

The Judges

Dr James 'JA' Cooper
is a writer, poet and educator. He is passionate about all of these, driving the Creative Writing and Communications program at Tabor and releasing a wealth of poetry and short stories for publication. He is also senior editor of *inScribe* journal. This was James's first time as a judge of *Stories of Life*. He was an inaugural member of the organising team and has been editor of the collection a number of times. This year, however, James has released his debut young adult novel, *Something About Alaska,* so he was charged with using all this skill and experience to assess the brilliant stories we received.

Lorraine Marwood
also loves writing for and sharing with young readers. She has published many poems for children in *The School Magazine* in NSW, six poetry collections for children, several reading books in educational series, four verse novels and many anthologised poems. Her verse novel *Star Jumps* won the inaugural Prime Minister's award for children's literature in 2010 and *Leave Taking* was a CBCA shortlisted book in 2019 and a winner in the NSW Patricia Wrightson award for children's fiction. Her latest book, *Footprints on the Moon,* is a CBCA Notable book for 2022. Lorraine was our judge in the short story category this year.

Contents

Introduction iv

The Judges vi

Things in Cages 1
   Gaynor Faulkner

An Unexpected Guest 6
   Jacqueline Waters

A Gift from God 8
   Emma Fisher

Precious Relics 11
   Jack Roney

Campfire Cathedral 13
   Karen Brough

I Can't Get My Head Around That 18
   Brian Morris

Trigger Moment 23
   Jo-Anne Berthelsen

Stop Holding on So Tight 28
   Dienece Darling

My Faith Tree 30
   Heather McMahon

Every Day is an Adventure 35
   Amy Bowden

A Call Away 40
   MJ Saladine

Wonderfully Made! 47
   Helena Stretton

Elections can be Dangerous 51
   Roslyn Bradshaw

Playing Hands 54
   Karen Curran

At Home in Lilliput 57
   Paula Vince

Not Alone 61
Rebekah Matson

The Minute 66
Jie Ni

Becoming Unmasked 71
Teri Kempe

Beauty Scars 73
Anastasia Korkodyllos

Plant a Seed 78
Dienece Darling

The Hand of God 83
Hazel Barker

My Dad 89
Ruth C Hall

An Unexpected Meeting 91
Francina Flemming

Outside the Fold 95
June Hopkins

Blue 100
Roslyn Bradshaw

The Test 106
Teri Kempe

Sparks of Grace 111
Tony Koch

Meeting the Light 113
Glenda Austin

Bones and Blue Eyes 116
RJ Rodda

Emerging from the Fog 120
Craig Chapman

Love and Lemon Cake 125
Steph Penny

The Battle for Libby 127
Ruth C Hall

Teenage Hangout 132
   Leah Grant

It's Really a Miracle 135
   Jenny Woolsey

Insight from a Blacksmith 141
   Craig Chapman

Is it Enough? 143
   Val Russell

The Long Road 149
   Liisa Grace-Baun

On the Job 154
   Steph Penny

The Wild Elephant that Obeyed the Lord 159
   Wendy Radford

Behind the Wall 161
   Esther Cremona

My Sister Amy 167
   Natalie Ingram

Things in Cages

Gaynor Faulkner

Today, I'm not thinking about anything at all with feathers on my daily walk. It's only my thoughts that trudge along the path with me. Cloying and sticky in the summer heat. *What have I done agreeing to move to the city?* I see my future yawn in front of me like an endless dusty road in the outback. Making new friends, I know, is not so easy now I'm older.

Covid will put an end to the hobbies I thought I'd pursue and the new groups I was going to join. It puts a full stop to most things – like nudging me out of the job I'd loved so much. Even though my heart isn't in it, I utter a prayer as I walk along asking that everything will work out with this move. But the prayer feels small and trapped.

I barely finish when a bird boldly hops right in front of me on the path. Still absorbed in my sorry thoughts, I attempt to navigate myself around it but it shuffles closer and closer to my feet like a newborn puppy seeking its mother.

I'm not much of a bird type of person. Not really – so I don't know why it's attaching itself to me. I like them though – from that lofty distance they belong to in the sky. I admire the fluorescent colours of some, the flying acumen of others. I love watching the beautiful ones and curse the aggressive ones. There's no way though you'd see me armed with binoculars and camera, squinting my way through scratchy scrubland trying to spy a *spangled drongo* or a *spotted pardalote*. That's just not me.

I believe the real beauty of birds is their super power – their gift of flight. How they gracefully glide and soar in the breeze. The way they swim synchronised ballet in the blue grey ocean of sky.

There's something of the ethereal in birds, I've always thought – something fey. But the magic dissipates for me when they're not allowed to fly freely. Boxed birds always make my heart heavy.

Cages remind me of Samorn, the old elephant at Adelaide Zoo that grew up with me and my generation. For thirty-five years, when she wasn't trudging kids around the zoo, Samorn existed alone in the orange dust of her enclosure. Her wrinkled foot was tethered to the ground by a fat, rusty chain. Year in and year out, Samorn rocked back and forth, back and forth with one foot. Her slight shuffle of freedom caused such a deep rut in the hard earth that it overflowed with water when it rained – as if the elephant was crying. Mum could never understand why I refused to linger around the old elephant. I didn't have the words when I was a child. I just knew I couldn't look into cages. Even then.

Thinking of freedom is what pulls most at my heart now as I watch the frantic little bird in front of me. Its hopping tells me it, too, is in a cage. Trapped because it can no longer fly.

The bird has yellow eyes. One of the aggressive types, I notice. A noisy miner. But this bird's eyes are fixed and look up at me pleadingly. They don't stare wildly at me as though it's bat-crazy like other noisy miners seem to do. They just look…sad.

Next thing, someone's walking past and the bird painstakingly shuffles into some nearby bushes. Once the coast is clear, it hops painfully back to me. I feel complicit in its need to survive now. When a cyclist whizzes past, I fan some leaves from a nearby branch to help conceal it. I notice then the line of ants trickling over its downy feathers. My heart melts as it blinks imploringly up at me through the leaves.

Suddenly, a woman's approaching us, pulling hard at the leash of a robust dog.

'There's a bird that can't fly in the bushes here,' I tell her. I feel compelled to explain why I'm hanging around the bushes stock-still in this scorching heat. I also want her to rein in her excitable dog.

Her expression is immediately kind and concerned. 'Oh, poor little thing', she says. 'And those ants aren't giving it a chance to survive in this sun, I see. I live just here so I'll try to get rid of those ants later.' I watch as she enters her front yard up ahead.

I appreciate her kindness, but my concern hasn't been completely allayed. What if the ant repellent makes the bird sicker? I fret. Racing back to our unit, I ask my husband to help me save it. 'Don't be silly!' he says. 'In today's heat, it's only going to die. Just leave it.' But I can't stand to see it die.

I grab some pellets of cat food and sprinkle them into a lid of water and sprint back to where I'd left it. I'm concerned that the heat has already taken its life, but thankfully, the bird's still alive. It feebly hops out from the bush a little to greet me. The ants steadfastly cling to it like vultures.

I have my mobile with me now and phone the bird rescue helpline to find out what to do. Arming myself with their instructions, I grab our cat carrier and tentatively attempt to capture it. A man from a nearby house sees my struggles and kindly assists me. I hold the cage precariously when it's captured and trudge home. My husband subsequently drives us to the nearest vet. I sigh in relief. Here, it will surely be nursed back to health.

But, when I phone the vet later to see how the bird is faring, I'm unprepared for what they tell me. The bird has been euthanised.

It was too weak to save. I don't say goodbye to the receptionist when I hang up because I'm afraid I might cry.

'At least you saved it from an agonising slow death by ants in this heat,' my sister Kathy soothes later when I express my sadness. 'It would still be there dying, even now.' But her words only offer my heart a little comfort.

The next day on my walk I see a young woman out the front of the house where the lady with the dog lived.

'Was it your mother yesterday that helped me with a lame bird?' I call out.

The girl approaches me. 'Yes. Mum mentioned that poor bird,' she says. I ask her to please pass on that the bird was put down. How sad I was. The girl looks disappointed too.

'I'm Lyla,' the girl says when I introduce myself. She has a friendly face. Kind and smiling like her mother's. We chat amiably for quite a while. It emerges that we share similar interests, like our faith and writing stories.

I feel so comfortable chatting with Lyla that I find myself saying out of the blue, 'I had to give up work mainly due to my health – a congenital lung disease. Not good when Covid's around.' For once I say it casually, without shame. I've always found it so much easier to reveal secrets to a stranger.

The girl looks startled for a second. Hesitant. As though I have just divulged a deep secret I know about her. 'Me too!' she finally says. She laughs incredulously. I get the impression that she too has found it difficult to share this version of herself. 'My health has affected my life as well,' she tells me. 'Encephalitis years ago and health problems ever since. It's affected my studies.

Relationships sometimes…Thank goodness I always have my writing. That never leaves me,' she says.

A young girl that loves writing. Incarcerated sometimes by illness. We look at each other and slowly shake our heads. It's as though we are old, dear friends that have suddenly recognised each other. Lyla is smiling and radiantly positive. I know how hard that sometimes can be. Suddenly, my problems seem small as a mouse.

Lyla and I plan to meet up soon to share our mutual enjoyment of writing. And just yesterday my husband and I saw the neighbour that helped me put the bird in the cage that day and we enjoyed a long friendly chat with him. Adelaide doesn't seem that lonely place I'd envisioned for my future now. It seems exciting and rich with possibilities.

I realised that day that compassion towards others transcends concerns for myself. I also learnt that even when my prayers seem miniscule and confined, God still hears, loud and clear. It took that little bird to show me that God doesn't see cages at all.

An Unexpected Guest

Jacqueline Waters

At 8.30am the telephone rang.

I had been fighting a virus all week and didn't feel like getting out of bed. I had the winter blues as well. There were too many weeds in the garden, too little warmth in the sun to dry the washing, no small wood to keep the fire burning, not enough time to work on my writing projects.

I remembered my grandson, Isaac, had promised to come over and give me a hand in the garden, so I forced myself to get out from under the warm quilt and into the frigid kitchen, and answered the phone. It was my daughter.

'Mum, would you like a newborn lamb to feed?'

Now, I love going over to their farm to feed the lambs, but this would be a commitment to three-hourly feeds between 7am and 10pm for the six days they would be away. I needed more sleep, not less. And I would have to postpone going out to lunch with my eldest granddaughter.

'It's one of twins and the mother has only one teat,' she went on. Left to its own devices, we both knew it would die. I couldn't bear the thought.

'Yes, okay,' I heard myself say.

'Thanks. Isaac can bring it over.'

Isaac arrived with a large cardboard box in the bottom of which a tiny lamb was curled, all hooves and knobbly knees.

'She hasn't had a feed yet,' he said.

Wow! I thought. *She really is brand-new.* I had never fed such a newborn. Isaac produced a bottle and teat, colostrum powder for the first day and milk power for after that. He showed me how to hold her between my legs, put my thumb in her mouth and introduce the teat through the space made. At least she sucked well. We put straw in the lamb shed and made the pen secure. I named her Maisie.

Two hours later I tried my hand at feeding her. She wriggled like crazy and resisted my attempts to get the teat in her mouth, but I prevailed, and five minutes later came away proud of my new prowess.

Four days later she was growing steadily. I enjoyed hearing her gentle bleating when she saw me coming with her feed. I didn't even mind getting up early and going out into the pre-dawn cold, or the last feed of the day at ten o'clock when I am usually tucked into a nice warm bed playing Wordle.

As Maisie looks up at me from between my knees and tugs hungrily on the teat, I reflect that my life has taken a turn for the better. I have given her life, and in return she has given me more to live for.

I wouldn't have said a newborn lamb was what I needed to shake off the winter blues, but sometimes life gives us what we need, not what we want.

A Gift from God
Emma Fisher

You know the feeling when God is working and you don't even know it? Do you know how you have to hit rock bottom in order to understand and accept the otherwise impossible? Well, this is my story.

I was a mum of three girls and doing the whole worldly thing without God, and I had just had a little boy. A week after a beautiful homebirth, things began to go wrong. His body was not quite working as it should. He started getting sleepy and sleeping with his eyes open. Thinking this was really odd, we took him to the doctors at a week old. Before we knew it, we were rushed off to the Lyell McEwin Hospital and then to Women's and Children's Hospital where he would spend the following six weeks.

After that night, I didn't get to spend much time with him. I found myself under investigation, with allegations by Child Protection Services that we had done something wrong to explain why he had become so ill. I spent the next few weeks under investigation while doctors worked to save my boy. Since I hadn't bonded with him the week he was home, nothing hit me at first. It was surreal, suddenly going from pregnant to a struggling new mum of now four children, and then this. One doctor said, 'He's more dehydrated than the Mexican babies who were stuck under rubble for three days,' which broke my heart completely. His sodium levels were through the roof. I was told there was no documentation of anything like this happening in the world. I struggled to get my head around any of it.

I spent over a week being constantly questioned. It felt like my house had been completely invaded. My phone was taken away as evidence, and I was juggling my girls, my house, hospital runs, a breaking relationship and my newborn son in a critical condition, while being treated like a criminal. It was awful.

At some point in this mess I asked people to send good vibes, pray, send well wishes and anything they believed would help. Prayer was a last resort. At some point in the quiet moments by my son's bedside, processing everything going on – bleeding on the brain from the swelling when he was re-hydrated when he first came into the hospital, and now how their smallest tubes were too big for his tiny delicate veins and a huge possibility of them collapsing under the stress of the work that needed to be done – God came. Thank God! He came and changed me. I don't even recall if I prayed, but someone did. He came back into my life, fully and unquestionably present.

I pondered these doctors working with my son, some who acted like they were miracle workers. But God was demonstrating his involvement. Unquestionably, God exists and he saved my son. He was *in* my son's veins that day…I am confident of this because some time later I saw a vision of God in my son's tiny little veins. God was standing with feet out strong, arms up high, holding up my boy's veins that day in the hospital.

Fast forward to today. My son is coming up to his second birthday, something I couldn't picture happening during that first month and a half of his life. I was cleared of any ill-intention. It turned out the dehydration was a combination of a genetic condition causing dry skin, coupled with a bit of jaundice and low breastmilk supply. After that time in hospital he never left my care. He is doing so well.

At six months old he was diagnosed with cerebral palsy on his left side, with the diagnosis sounding quite bad...but God. God can do amazing things. The only thing my son was struggling with was walking, and he's catching up with the help of an amazing physiotherapist. He has been an independent walker from the age of eighteen months and we are looking into orthotics to help set his feet, leg muscles and hips correctly. But that's it. From such a rough beginning to this amazing, pudgy little boy who is funny, smart, and catching up fast. You would have no idea looking at him about his struggles and start in life, the severity of his beginnings.

But I will never forget. He is my gracious gift from God. Every moment I look at him I find myself staring in wonder. Naming him was a battle during pregnancy. I originally wanted to call him William (meaning 'determined protector') but his dad argued against that name, and when he was born I took heed and named him Matthew. After all the drama ended, I looked up his name: 'gift from God'; indeed he is, and I am so blessed. His name is Matthew William, and he is a gift from God first, and determined protector second. And he is living up to his name.

Precious Relics

Jack Roney

Jack was a butcher. A blue collar, meat-and-three-veg, kind of bloke. Humble and quietly spoken, never an ill word passed his lips. He was a man of faith, gentle and kind, honest and hardworking, a dedicated father and husband, a small man with a huge heart.

Christened John Terrance, his parents and eight siblings called him Jack. Why not John? I don't have the foggiest. Like his sister Kathy whom they called Maude, and his other sister Elizabeth whom they called Betty. I guess it was just what they did in those days, the good old days when he rode his horse to school, barefoot with a tin lunchbox slung over his shoulder by a strap fashioned from twine, rope threaded through the hoops of his shorts where a leather belt should have been. His family left the rolling pastures of the Ravensbourne highlands to rebuild their lives in the city. Doing his bit to support the family, he left school bound for the meatworks where he completed his apprenticeship.

My earliest memory of Jack, the man my two brothers, sister and I called Dad, was of him standing proudly behind the counter of his own butcher shop, draped in a striped apron over a starched white shirt and bowtie, black hair combed with a side part and slicked with oil, and Elvis-like muttonchop sideburns, smile beaming as he wrapped sausages, prime rump or chuck steak in sheets of brown paper sliced from a humungous roll. He knew all the customers' names and preferred cuts. An aluminium holster dangled from his belt, large enough to hold half a dozen knives and a honing steel. He was a whiz at sharpening blades, but he admitted it was a miracle he still had all ten fingers.

'You'll be with God soon, Dad,' I said, as I leaned over him in the hospital bed. I stroked his thinning grey hair and kissed his forehead. His eye lines told of warm smiles and affection, of a man who had traversed life over eight decades. Yet the creases between his brows told of worries past, regret and a troubled mind.

'I know, son,' he whispered. The storm in his mind quelled. Eternal peace followed.

He cherished those knives. They were handed down to me, precious relics. I will be their custodian until I pass them down to my sons.

Jack is in every fibre of my being. I feel his presence, subtle reminders that his DNA flows through my veins. I see him in my shadow, the way I hunch my shoulders just as he did. I see him when I catch my reflection in storefront windows. I see his hands when I hold mine up against a blue sky. Freckled knuckles, stumpy fingers, and sun-mottled skin.

In my mind's eye, I'm still youthful – but the mirror tells me otherwise. I study my face, battered by weather, wrinkles emerging. I smile. Jack smiles back at me. He is still here with me.

Campfire Cathedral

Karen Brough

He'd arrived at 8am sharp.

A cool wintry Melbourne morning. Being so early, the brain fog was like an old Holden ute: the key clicks, engine gasps, trying to finally turn over and spark to life – struggling to awaken.

Bed hair. Body weary, I sat at the kitchen table, eating some poached eggs and pears, trying to replenish after a task-heavy week. Desperately needing some good, uninterrupted sleep and people-free days. Today this was not an option.

Here he was, the firebox man. John. Thick brown slightly wavy hair, late twenties, lanky, with kind eyes and a warm smile. Friendly, and as it turns out, an absolute master in the installation of woodfire boxes.

Complaints tattered off like machine gun rapid fire within my mind. *I don't feel like having people in my home, Lord. I wish this wasn't happening today. I want to switch off for a bit, from noise and people. The calendar has been so full, I just need a day's reprieve. Please let him go about his day and let me do mine.*

John, with his tile cutting tools, drills and hammers, working away in the background. The sound reverberated throughout the house.

He's in my space – the space where my head needs peace and quiet.

John went about his work over the course of the morning. Laying the hearth, positioning the soon to be sweet little wood box for lazy, toasty Sunday afternoons.

Aaahhh, won't that be lovely, as I dreamt of 'no rush', no scurry, agenda-free time being warmed by the fire. Before I knew it, midday had arrived; lunchtime.

John gingerly knocked on the door and entered the house.

'Could I borrow some water, please?' holding up his two-minute noodle cup with a friendly grin.

Mood improved, I laughingly responded, 'I can do better than that. You can have some!' As the kettle boiled, he sat on the kitchen stool behind the bench, and we started chatting like old friends. No topics were off the agenda for John; he was proving to be a curious and thoughtful fella. The clocks hands moved quickly past the hour.

Before I knew it, the subject of God came up.

The kettle bubbled and boiled and eventually clicked, alerting me it had finished its job. Pouring the water into the noodle cup, the conversation continued to roll with ease.

A wide grin spread across his lips. 'You sound like my wife,' he casually commented.

'How is that?' I enquired.

'Oh, you know, she goes to church sometimes. She's religious, like you.'

Without skipping a beat, I responded, 'I don't really consider myself religious, actually.'

He looked at me, questioning what this meant.

'I consider myself more "spiritual". Religious, to me, means a whole lot of rules and regulations but, for me, spiritual is relational. My relationship with God is just that. A friendship. I talk to him about the things going on in my life, and then I listen to what he might want to say to me. He talks to us all in our own ways. Ways we understand.'

He nodded. 'I think my wife is like that,' adding, 'I don't think I'm that spiritual either. I'm just not made that way, I suppose.' His eyes dropped to the floor, downcast as the words left his lips.

My spirit grieved at his last comment; like a thorn, it panged in my heart.

Oh Lord, Lord. This is so wrong. He is spiritual. Please don't let him leave without meeting you.

'What kind of things make your wife spiritual?' I asked, offering a fork to John now that his noodles were brewing.

He took the fork from my hand and stirred the noodles as they softened inside the cup. 'My wife, she kneels by her bed each night and prays with her hands together. I just leave her be when she's like that.'

Maybe he's not meant to be like his wife.

That's right! He's not meant to be like her.

The penny dropped. *He thinks being spiritual is about kneeling to pray, leadlight windows and men in funny outfits chanting in large cathedrals.*

My spirit leapt about, as this light-bulb epiphany zipped in. 'John, maybe you're not meant to be like your wife.'

He laughed and said, 'You got that right! What do you mean, though?'

A picture of John popped into my mind's eye. He was in the middle of the bush, surrounded by scrub and large gum trees. They overhung the smoky fire which had been burning all night. John sat in the early hours of the morning, in his camp chair. Hot drink in mug, warming his hands as he sat watching the flicker of flames. He was alone, as the thick morning mist and brisk air hung about. Motorbikes sat in the background and half a dozen tents encircled the campfire.

I watched in the picture, as John looked around at the surroundings, appreciating nature and its beauty. Listening. Looking. Taking in the peace and enjoying the quiet. Holy ground for John.

This is John's cathedral! Oh Lord, Lord, thank you! This is amazing!

I shared the picture with him. 'What if God speaks to you while you're in the bush, enjoying some motorbiking with mates? Sitting by the fire, appreciating the beautiful surroundings. What if this is how he connects with you, John?'

His eyes grew wide with delight. 'That's my kind of church!' he cheered.

All went silent for a moment or two, as he processed this idea, turning it over in his mind. I could almost see the cogs turning, as he stirred the now soft noodles, almost ready to eat.

His eyes widened with amazement as the picture I'd described rang true. 'How did you know that? I *do* like camping and motorbiking.'

Oh Lord, you are AMAZING. Thank you.

'I *do* sit by the campfire in the bush and look at what's around me. I love it. I go all the time and it's just like that. That's amazing. How did you know that?'

My eyes teared up a little, as I saw John being wowed.

'That's God, John. He is the only one who could have known that. You know that I can't have known that. I don't think you coming here today was a mistake. He wanted you to know how much he wants to talk with you.' I quickly added, 'And to tell you it's okay that you're not like your wife.'

We both laughed.

'I like that. I reckon you might be right,' he responded thoughtfully.

John went outside not long after, having consumed the noodles and been encouraged by God through a personal picture of his life. He laid the hearth, cut the holes in the roof and ceiling, and positioned the flue. He moved the firebox into position and sealed it all up. Throughout the afternoon, he would occasionally poke his head in and ask another question or make another comment. Never had a tradesman done such an honourable job in our home. What a gift the day had been.

No, it wasn't what I'd felt like today. I had wanted to remain in my own little world, but God had other ideas. I could have shut him out. I could have said no, but what an adventure I'd have missed out on if I had.

By the end of the day John had cleaned up every speck of mess, collected his tools, waved goodbye, and headed home to 'tell his wife all about it'.

Hubby Craig and I snuggled in front of our new little firebox. It was cosy warm. I shared what God had done with the day. A day where I'd chosen to say yes, and the problems of my world shrank because of God growing in John's.

I Can't Get My Head Around That

Brian Morris

'Whitefellas are too keen to disown the wisdom of the body, mistaking our loss of receptivity for maturity' – Tim Winton, with reference to the observations of aboriginal philosophers David Mowaljarlai and Bill Neidjie

Until recently I never knew that the body is important for life. I don't mean physical life. I mean relational and spiritual life. I am on a journey now of connecting with my body. But this journey began half a lifetime ago.

I liked preaching…or so I thought. What I actually liked was the sense of power and influence it gave, and the accolades and approval that came after I preached. Accolades and approval were signs that I had done a good job. They helped establish my identity as being someone worthwhile by doing something that is regarded as worthwhile.

I was in my third pastorate, at a church in regional Victoria. About one year into this pastorate, I conducted a series of sermons preached over three Sundays. I had not prepared the final sermon as well as I would have liked. As I approached the pulpit to preach, I got the usual adrenalin rush of stepping into a place of influence and power. There was something else going on in my body too. I ignored it.

Halfway through the sermon, I couldn't recall points I had committed to memory. I scrambled to find a place in my notes where I could go to bring the sermon back on track. I couldn't find a place quick enough. The feeling I had ignored in my body was increasing, a rising foreboding, wraithlike, warning me of something. My head thought, *I don't know what I am doing here or where this sermon is going.*

I managed to close off the sermon quickly and end the worship service. I headed for the exit where I said goodbye to the people who attended. I wanted redemptive accolades and approval of the sermon. None came. Just the neutral 'goodbyes' and 'thank yous' that are etched into people's habits of politeness. My head interpreted this lack of approving response as *I have failed. While being nice and polite when leaving, the people are really taken aback by the sermon's failure. I have made a fool of myself.*

The feeling of wraithlike foreboding in my body was changing shape. It had turned into a two-sided feeling. One part was protective: *you need to go and hide now.* I couldn't get home quick enough to do just that – to a safe place. The other part of the feeling had more intensity. Which is strange, because this part of the feeling felt like I was gutted, emptied of any sense of self. If nothingness can be felt, then that is what I was feeling. Maybe that is the beginning of bodily awareness, to notice such a disembodied state. I was an empty shell, a haunted house where people do not live, as the ghosts of the past may terrify and destroy. Such a vulnerable state.

This feeling in my body was overpowering; it could not be ignored. My head said the feeling was about me being a failure, a fool in front of all those people. My body did not offer any interpretation. It just felt. Only in retrospect have I understood something of what was happening. My body was gutting me of an identity which had been built on getting accolades and approval for doing things regarded as worthwhile, which then made me someone worthwhile.

The building of a different identity was soon to begin. An identity not based in the so-called importance of one's work and the performance of such, or in other people's opinions. An identity embedded in a bodily received knowledge of grace. My head did not have a clue about this bodily knowledge.

The Wednesday night after the Sunday, my wife and I went out for dinner with a couple, Paul and Sue, who were friends. They were safe enough for me not to hide. If I needed to hide, I could put on a cheery face, and not let them see this strange feeling in my body, or so I thought. A few minutes into the evening Paul casually said, 'Thanks, Brian, for your sermon last Sunday, I appreciated your thoughts.'

I was stuck in no man's land. It was too late for my need for accolades and approval to be satisfied, and I knew darn well that the sermon was crap. *What should I say?* My face grimaced as it went red, and I fumbled around in my head for a response. Before I could say anything, Paul, being an intuitive man, must have picked up on my hesitation to respond and my facial expression, and said, 'I am flying down to Apollo Bay on Saturday to get my hours up. Do you want to come along?' That helped. Being a person who loved aeroplanes, I didn't hesitate to reply in the affirmative.

Apollo Bay is about an hour's flying time south of where we lived. We intended to fly down, walk the two kilometres into the town from the airstrip, have lunch and return by late afternoon. However, on the day, the plane was not available until after lunch. We could still get down to Apollo Bay, get a quick coffee, and return home in time.

As we took off and headed to Apollo Bay, my body was registering something other than emptiness. I was beginning to notice 'stuff' happening in my body that I had not recognised before. There was a light-heartedness that so often comes with play for the sake of play. For most of my life, play was serious, about competing and winning. The bodily feeling I had on the way to Apollo Bay was a playful, buoyant feeling, without being adrenaline-charged.

We landed in Apollo Bay and walked into town, enjoying the stunning scenery of that place, chatting about aeroplanes, football, and other nicely neutral things. Not church, sermons, or work. We forgot about time.

Halfway through the coffee I looked at my watch and asked, 'What time do we have to be back home?'

Paul looked at his watch and, with a panic-ridden stare in his eyes, said, 'Oh no!' (and a few other choice words). 'We have to be off the ground in twenty minutes otherwise we won't be back before last light, and we'll be staying here tonight. I don't have a night licence.'

Not that I minded the prospect of staying in Apollo Bay for the night; and the next day was Sunday. I was happy to skip Sundays now.

'Why?' I asked. 'What is the problem? Is there something you have to get back for? We can ring and let them know we are coming back tomorrow.'

'Well, that would be nice,' Paul said. 'But we don't know what the weather is going to be like tomorrow.' (It was the south coast of Victoria, after all.) 'And I have only got the plane for today.'

'Stuff it. We are in trouble then. We'd better run.'

And run we did. All the way back to the airstrip. Something else was happening amidst the rush to return to the plane. We both began to laugh at the crazy predicament we had got ourselves into. These were 'belly' laughs. Not laughs that come because our mind appreciates a funny joke. There was a visceral connection between Paul and myself. If I was on my own, I would have been in my head, thinking about time, worrying, and getting angry for being so forgetful. Instead, because we were together, we laughed – no head logic; just ran, and laughed at this situation we were in. We laughed and puffed our way back to the plane. We took off from Apollo Bay in time to beat the last light of the day home.

Seated beside my friend as he flew the plane, I began to get further strange feelings inside my body. There was a tenderness toward him. A vulnerable feeling of powerless gratitude and affection. These vulnerable bodily feelings can be disturbing for a man who has been enculturated into manhood as having to live from his head. They are a threat to his identity as a man. But my body did not know about that threat.

Somewhere in the day with Paul, my body had registered, like it never had before, that this man was doing something caring for me without any conditions attached. The balmy warmth of affection that comes from being with someone who just likes being with you. I had not recognised this feeling before in my life. The psychic, spiritual rupture between my head and body had been cavernous. My head had deceived me into thinking, and believing, that to know something in my head was all there is to knowledge and maturing as a person. My body was beginning to lead me to a more abundant, grace-experienced life as an embodied human being. Something I still struggle to get my head around.

Trigger Moment

Jo-Anne Berthelsen

I cannot believe it has come to this. I sit and watch, heart in mouth, as the wigmaker snips off the final, few strands of hair still clinging to our daughter's scalp, in order to begin the process of creating a personalised wig for her. Our girl has been so brave, but now she cannot contain her grief. When those last, fragile vestiges of hope fall to the floor, she sobs, heartbroken.

As I move to comfort her, I notice how even the experienced wigmaker is turning away, eyes filled with tears. Yet I know I must be strong for our daughter, so I hold her close and try my best to comfort her. I tell her she is still beautiful. I tell her we love her so much. And I tell her that, when she has her special wig, no one will know.

Since her mid-teens, she has had to cope with a disease that affects her energy levels and general wellbeing and dictates what she can and cannot eat. At times, she is so debilitated, but she tries her best to keep going, always thoughtful, always caring. Yet, worse than the disease itself is her devastating hair loss.

At first, only a small clump disappears here and there. And at first, the hair grows back. Later, our daughter tries a painful treatment that bears no positive result and she soon becomes adept at hairstyles that hide her loss. Yet such efforts eventually prove fruitless. Week by week, the bare patches grow wider and wider and, every few days, she watches, anguished, as piles of hair float away in the shower. 'It's not fair!' she sometimes sobs, when it all becomes too much for her.

She marries young and, with her wedding fast approaching, chooses a pretty hat to wear that hides those large, bare patches. Yet soon even this special hat is inadequate, so another is found. On the day, she carefully arranges thin strands of her hair across her forehead and around her neck. She looks beautiful. Everyone celebrates with her – and some who know also applaud her courage.

In the months ahead, her precious hair keeps on disappearing and, one day, she finally decides to visit an experienced wigmaker in the city. She asks me to come with her and, of course, I agree. I would do anything to support her. Yet it is hard to watch such devastation – so very hard.

After our day in the city, she struggles on, confronting other huge challenges in her life. Yet, through it all, she manages to hold her head high and soldier on, armed with a variety of wigs to suit her mood. We support her as best we can, but realise she is strong enough to make her own choices now. She is brave and resilient, yet I cannot seem to forget that devastating moment with her in the city when those final strands of hair were removed. That day, she was my little girl needing such comfort and reassurance. That day, I so much longed to make everything right for her.

The years pass. Then, one evening, I find myself again watching, heart in mouth, as strands of hair fall to the floor. This time it is my husband's hair. He is seated on the front platform in our church, a little embarrassed but still smiling. As one of our pastors, he has agreed to have his head shaved, to raise money for a young woman in our congregation involved in overseas mission work. Who would have thought my husband's fine, reasonably sparse hair would ever be the focus of so much attention?

Everyone has insisted I sit right in the front row to watch this spectacle. Behind me, others are clapping and cheering, yet I find I cannot join in. As I watch, in an instant, I am thrust back to another time and place altogether. With one whirr of that shiny, silver shaver, I am once again in the wigmaker's room in the city – and I am devastated.

To my horror, I begin to cry. I have nowhere to hide, seated where I am. I try to hold back my tears, yet now, all those years later, they tumble down my cheeks in torrents, as if a dam has burst inside me. I sit as still as possible, endeavouring not to draw attention to myself. I am glad everyone else seems focussed on the strange sight of my husband with half his hair reduced to mere stubble. Yet, as those on the platform pause for a photo, one or two friends notice my tears and assume I am upset for my husband's sake – or perhaps my own.

When they enquire, I shake my head and try to smile. I know my husband wants to do this and that his hair will grow again. I thank them for their concern, but cannot tell them what is happening inside me. I do not understand it fully myself, but I know how I feel. It is as if I am standing on the edge of a vast chasm, watching helpless and horrified, while a young woman tumbles into its depths like a rag doll. The young woman is our daughter – and those bitter tears I cry are for our beautiful, brave girl, so broken and bereft, that day in the city.

As I continue to watch more of my husband's hair float to the floor, I am unprepared for the rush of anguish that begins to assault every part of me. Again and again, with every snip of the scissors and whirr of that shiny shaver, I see those last few strands of our daughter's hair falling, falling and hear her heartbroken sobs.

Many times over the years, we prayed for her healing, begging God to strengthen her body, to cause her hair to grow back, to show us the right treatment for her. Others, too, placed loving hands on her and prayed for her, but the healing did not come. In the end, she lost her hair – even those last, few, precious strands. Yet now my husband is voluntarily giving his up. What I am witnessing in this moment seems so incongruent with the vivid images flashing before my eyes that I cannot reconcile the two.

I am angry. I want to scream out that losing one's hair is no light matter, that it can be so painful and wounding – but I stay silent, overwhelmed with grief.

The rest of the evening's events continue on around me with much noise and hilarity. A trivia quiz is organised, but I want no part in it. My mind is whirling, yet I try to appear normal as I search for a quiet place to sit and regroup. I am still teetering, aghast, on the edge of that huge, dark chasm inside me and cannot take in anything that is said – even the announcement of the large amount of money my husband's 'Shear the Shepherd' effort has raised. All I want to do is go home and hide.

In the following days and weeks, as I seek to process my devastating trigger moment further, at last I begin to discern the gracious hand of God in it all. I did not know how traumatic such moments could be for those thrust back into the most horrendous life events imaginable in an instant. Now I understand, to some degree at least, and can empathise more. But beyond that, I see now how God enabled me to be strong when I needed to be strong for our daughter's sake and to grieve when the time was right for me. I see such grace and mercy in this and I am grateful.

I still grieve for our girl. I still do not understand fully why God has not answered our prayers for her healing. Yet, as she continues to strive and grow in her life, I am beginning to see how all the pain she has experienced enables her to notice others' pain much more readily, to care more deeply than so many of us do, to reach out and help her friends as best she can. Through her own suffering, she has learnt to love her neighbour well, just as Jesus taught us to do – and to love herself more in the process.

I thank God for her. And I am so proud of her, so very proud.

Stop Holding on So Tight

Dienece Darling

'It's time to go,' I say, even though we probably haven't been here a full minute. There's just something about a string of hot days that zaps a mother's patience.

Two brown heads bend over the dual steering wheel of the play-to-ride, Jurassic-style truck in the middle of a shopping centre walkway, as if they didn't hear me. I am not fooled, but I hold onto my patience and step closer. 'It's time to go.' The oldest grumbles but starts to obey.

The youngest doggedly keeps his head down and jerks the steering wheel with gusto. Why couldn't he just listen? His dad and I had whispered about taking them to the ice cream shop as a surprise after this. Now I'm thinking I can't reward bad behaviour. But then, we have been aimlessly walking around the air-conditioned shops to escape the heat. He has got to be bored and tired out of his mind. I certainly am.

I give him another chance. Walking to his side, bending over, calling his name, and taking his arm, I repeat the message. The pretence of ignorance dissolves. He throws back his head in an overheated tantrum that snaps the last thread of my patience. Well, at least it's obvious. We're not going to the ice cream shop.

My temper flares. *He ought not to assume the worst of things. Change doesn't have to be scary. He needs to trust me. Sometimes I have a special surprise planned – like today.*

Rather pleased with what I've decided is a sparkling gem of wisdom, I begin to bend down to share it with my son.

The words never pass my lips. Instead, they slam into my own grumbling heart.

My church just split. Friends have walked away. My ministry dissolved, and to top it off, my local Coles – my refuge and escape through all the long, dark Covid lockdowns – is being forced to close. Everything is changing, and I hate it.

Maybe I'm the one holding on too tight, thinking only the worst of change. What if God is up there saying, 'I was going to take you to the ice cream shop next'? And he's just waiting for me to trust him.

Alright, God. It's half prayer, half self-chastisement. *I'll trust you with the future.*

I finish bending over. 'You need to obey Mummy the first time' are the words that actually come out of my mouth because my son is four. Even my eleven-year-old would look at me askance if I told him he ought not to assume the worst of change. No, that message came straight from God for this resistant-to-change mother.

I take my boys to the ice cream shop because sometimes we all need a smattering of grace when we have trouble letting go of what we love for something we can't see in the future.

My Faith Tree

Heather McMahon

My life is like a house, with rooms added as events happened and as time goes on. I would love to share my story through an open inspection; however, I need to draw attention to the slab first.

Mum and Dad started building my foundation with the right materials but, alas, over a short time it began to crack. As you can imagine, this did not create secure living conditions –always in fear of movement under your feet that might give way at any time. I mean, really, how can one grow and learn when their mind is always occupied with that? This is the house I was given. It was no one's fault.

I am grateful that Mum planted a seed early on in one of those cracks, so as I lead you through the front door into the main living room, here it stands in the very centre, thick and wide. It is the heart of my house and it is alive. As it grew from a seed it pushed through the crack in the floor and as the roots spread throughout the foundations, it actually stabilised the floors, and its canopy spread wide and thick over the top. This is my faith tree.

When I was nine, I made a promise to acknowledge my faith tree's purpose and presence in me, which was hope and peace. As I was the only child of my parents, I took great comfort in its existence as well as the blessings it attracted in the forms of singing birds and fluttering butterflies, drawn towards the tree's sweet-scented white flowers. It gave me the strength I needed. There is no roof; I would always be incomplete if it were not for the protection of my faith tree. My house is quite plain from the front but considering there was a tree growing from the inside out, to some it was very odd and was mocked.

My Faith Tree

  The front room of my house is not a room I choose to enter often, due to the cracked walls, patched-up curtains and peeling paint. This room was built when I was young and its window faced the main street. People could look right in. Mum and Dad used to fight in here. The curtains were ripped in their battles. I've tried to mend them the best I could.

  I always loved that hanging mirror on the wall; it's a shame it got broken. Its golden curvy frame reminds me of the story of Snow White when the witch became jealous. Very apt, I feel, considering there were actually three adults involved in this battle. When the curtains were ripped, there were cruel spectators watching, many informing me of things I didn't need to know. The weather was always cold and stormy on those nights. Thank goodness for my tree. There was a hollow in its trunk where I could be warm and safe. During this time my tree was everything to me – it was my comfort and shelter. It was the most important presence in my childhood, which is the reason I built the next room.

  There are no windows in here. They weren't necessary as the outside world was irrelevant to me. Everything in this room is in honour of my tree. Above the bed is a branch that I broke off from it and mounted to the wall. It reminds me that it is always present from the moment I go to sleep to the moment I wake up. I painted the picture of my Faith Tree, hanging it on the opposite wall, to express how much it means to me. On the bedside table, which is made from its wood, sits a tealight candle made from its sap and crushed flora. When lit, it emanates an aroma of sweet-scented flowers which fills the room. Yet another reminder that I am enwrapped in its peace, like a spiritual blanket. I keep the door to this room open to remind myself to visit often.

This next room was built while Dad went out fishing one weekend when I was about fifteen. My mum made a choice to leave him, taking the furniture too. The root runners of my tree grow against the walls and are strong enough to hold onto and there are exposed roots about floor level to walk along to the other side, as the floor is gone. Apart from the cold, there is a wind in here that is very strong and whirls up and down like a tornado. I guess it's hardly a room anymore but this is where my life changed completely. There was nothing left but a devastating emptiness in my family. It had to happen, and it is a room I could do without, yet it's a room that should have been substantial. It has created great weakness in the whole structure of my house. Thankfully, I have my tree to hold things together.

Moving to another city was like the calm after the storm, like stepping outside and inhaling the fresh scent of pine in the air and a feeling of the golden warmth of a new day penetrating my skin as I exhaled a smile of relief. The expanse of blue sky calmed my spirit to infinite heights.

Back inside, now recharged, we follow a corridor. This is where I continue my education. Looking down, there are root runners flowing along with me. At the end of the corridor there are three closed doors, one on each side. Now, you would think that a right-handed person like myself would naturally choose either the door to the right or straight ahead. The choice I made changed me.

I saw a lot of potential renovation that could be done in this next room and for some reason I thought I would be the one to do it. It is dark and musty and you can smell sweaty shoes and a weedy scent. I didn't become a part of this room but I gave into the cracks of its weakness. The roots in here are thin and rubbery and not strong enough to hold the foundations together. I got stuck in some of the cracked foundations. A little surprise caused me to reconsider: a flower grew. It helped motivate me to accept that, as a single mother at eighteen, I should leave this room to give my flower better, more natural light to grow. It was hard because I felt the tugging of loyalty to the room to make it a better place but, in the end, I could see the roots dying in there.

When I stepped out, I possessed a chain around my ankle coming from that room; every now and then I was pulled back in. That is, until I found a rope hanging from inside the doorway of another room across from this one. I grabbed this hanging rope and swung myself and my flower into this room. Some people would say that I entered it too quickly but, when the door slammed, it cut off the chain.

It's a lovely warm room, with soft burgundy velvet chairs, red roses, a strong flickering fireplace when the rain is pouring outside, and a beautiful view from the window overlooking the garden. Reclaiming my conscience, everything became stable again. The conditions were so good that my flower multiplied and made three – I met my husband here.

A staircase was built in there, taking my house to a whole new level and a new room – one different to any before. Lots of chairs and dining tables, and reflections of candle light flickering on shimmering glassware and sparkling cutlery, regimentally placed upon crisp white cloths and sharp white napkins. The roots of my faith tree run along the floor up here, not as dense as below but still present.

Champagne anyone? Congratulations to the new hosts with clinking glasses – buzzing, orderly chaos. Cooking, tasting and waiting on diners. Smooth creamy smoked chicken fettuccini with a zing of sun-dried tomatoes, and the sizzling aroma of hot buttered prawns, garlic and sweet chilli. Warm, soul-satisfying comfort food.

As time progressed, though, things began to falter. Candles blew out from cold draughts coming through cracks in the walls, and there was less protection from my tree's canopy. Weathered bricks and crumbling mortar. There is a frustrated hole in the kitchen door and an angry broken window. It just gets worse the further we move to the end of this room. Pictures fallen off walls, empty wine bottles and broken glass. A pool of blood on the floor. Some birds flew in at times, creating some calm, and my flowers became climbers. They followed my faith tree's roots outside this room into their own ground. Butterflies flew in and showed me hope beyond this room, and that's when I built a door to walk out and get some fresh air.

As I stand at this door, I see the sea and sky before me, knowing that there are many more rooms that are yet to be built. It has been my privilege and pride to share with you the tree, my faith tree, that holds my house together.

Every Day is an Adventure

Amy Bowden

I look at my life and think, 'How on earth did I get here?' My family and I live in Mwanza, Tanzania, with four kids under four.

Our eldest, Boaz, is three years old. He's an energetic toddler, often called stubborn by fellow Africans. Boaz is brave and willing to explore new things and places. He is that kid who makes friends wherever he goes. His white blond hair and big blue eyes attract much attention, which he doesn't seem to take much notice of.

Our second child is Louise. She is also three; no, they are not twins. Louise is Ugandan and became a part of our family when she was just five weeks old. Louise has a big personality. She is creative, extremely agile, loves art and music, and cannot sit still even for a moment.

As if our hands weren't full enough already with two little ones so close in age, we made the decision to have another child. My husband, Brett, will tell you that I wanted to have one more and put pressure on him as my clock was ticking, and that I was fearful that it would take a long time to conceive again. Little did we know that after three months of trying, I would fall pregnant with twins. To tell you the truth, fertility was an issue for me. I remember when I was in my teens and a gynaecologist diagnosed me with Poly Cystic Ovarian Syndrome and said it would be extremely difficult to fall pregnant; I was absolutely devastated to hear this. I had always wanted to be a mum and have a family of my own.

When I was twenty years old, I came back to God after years of separation and some traumatic events that shaped my life. I found myself entering a church and having a real and meaningful relationship with God which I had never experienced before.

Brett and I met when I was twenty-nine years old. We dated for three months and then got engaged. I know it was a short courtship but when you know, you know, right? We were old enough to have some life experience under our belt to help us navigate married life. At our engagement party a family friend invited us to travel to Uganda with her on a mission trip. So we went to Uganda for our honeymoon. One night while sleeping on the floor of the children's home with mice running everywhere, the thought of being on some glamorous beach resort honeymoon did cross my mind, but I knew deep down that God had called us to Uganda and my heart was drawn to help these children and this community.

On our second visit to Uganda in 2016 we visited many churches. I was asked to speak at a pastors' conference. God put it on my heart to share a small part of our infertility journey. It was real, it was raw. I cried as I shared. I know God used this painful part of my journey to be an encouragement. I was standing in a room filled with people who knew what pain and suffering was. Every day was a struggle to feed and care for their families while ministering to their community with high expectations and little or no wage. I could see hearts touched as I spoke. At the end of the service one of the pastors asked if they could pray for us. I remember the fervent prayers and faith of those pastors. Later I found out that they were praying I would have twins. I laughed, thinking if I can't even have one child, how on earth would I have twins! To this day I still think about those prayers that charged the heavens and brought forth my family and all that we are today. The next month we found out I was pregnant. We were elated to bring our baby Boaz into this world.

Just three months after his birth another life changing moment happened. I was driving with Boaz and we had a seven-hour journey. We were only one hour in, and he was screaming and unhappy about being in the car and I was praying and struggling. Eventually he slept, and that was when I felt God speak to me. He told me to pull over the car. I did. I felt him ask, 'Would you be willing to adopt a child from Uganda?' I said yes. It's not very often in my life that I have heard an audible voice or a deep sense of calling and purpose, but I can say without a doubt this was a life changing moment for us. Later that night I received a message from the children's home director that a baby had been abandoned after her mother passed away in delivery. This had never happened before - normally only school age children were brought to the home. The baby was named Amy Louise by an Australian friend; I knew the moment I saw her photo that she was meant to be my daughter.

In 2019 we moved to Uganda. We sold everything, including our house, and used the money to build infrastructure at the school which we had been supporting since our first mission trip, and to support ourselves. When this ran out, Brett had to look for work, which God provided in neighbouring Tanzania at the start of 2020.

Fast forward to May 2020. After years of processing, we had adopted our daughter, now called Louise. We were continuing the work at the school and the children's home. I was now pregnant with the twins. Uganda was in complete lockdown due to Covid, we were stuck, unable to return to Australia to deliver (as originally planned), unable to get Louise a passport so she could travel, unable to leave our compound.

Brett had been travelling in and out of Uganda to work; however, he was stuck in Uganda due to border closures. Some issues arose with one of the twins *in utero*, so we were forced to make the gut-wrenching decision to separate our family to get the medical care our unborn child needed. As I was pregnant, we got a letter granting us permission on medical grounds to leave Uganda and drive to Tanzania where we could get a flight to Australia. This was no small feat and took weeks of liaising and getting required documents. At this time you were not allowed to leave your compound by car. The city of Kampala was filled with police and army checkpoints, and cars were impounded daily for driving during the lockdown. All government offices were closed due to the lockdown, and we were unable to get a passport for Louise. We enrolled her in a boarding school run by an Australian friend.

Brett and I drove across the border to Tanzania where Boaz and I flew back to Australia so I could deliver our twins with safe and reliable medical care. Brett returned to work. It was not an easy time to travel with Covid. We had to get permission, with the help of my mum and her local member of parliament, to return to South Australia, my home state. I had to complete hotel quarantine with a toddler, which was challenging. I even made the news: 'Pregnant woman rushed to hospital to receive treatment' was the headline. I cried more tears in this time than I ever have before. I cried out to God for my children, all four of them. God heard my cry. The twin whom the doctors thought would not make it, or if he did would be disabled, is now a happy, healthy six-month-old. Though small, he is a fighter. We called him Benjamin because he 'sits at the right hand of God'. His sister is Annabelle. She too is healthy and strong.

Delivering our twins without my husband was terrifying. My sister was there with me through it all and I also know God was with me. Brett met the twins when they were eleven weeks old.

When the twins were four months old and we were all cleared to travel, I returned to Uganda to collect our daughter with my dad. It was a great battle, with many trips to government offices. We changed Louise's name so she carries our surname and got her a passport. We spent some time with her biological father, whom we had built a relationship with throughout the adoption process. We visited his home in a small village where Louise met with her biological family once again. We then relocated to Mwanza in Tanzania. Finally, our whole family was in one country. So here I am in our home in Mwanza with our four children under four, exhausted but with a heart full of love, in awe at how God brought us all together despite the obstacles we faced.

A Call Away

MJ Saladine

Kaitlyn Jones awoke with the same empty feeling in her stomach. *Another pointless day.* She sat up in her tangled sheets, feeling flustered and bothered, then leaned to her bedside table to check the time on her phone.

11:55am. 'Time for lunch, but I'm not hungry,' Kaitlyn whispered.

A scratching noise came from the door.

Maisy.

Rolling her eyes, she stood up and walked to open the door. Kaitlyn found her golden retriever sitting there panting with excitement. Maisy barked, wagging her tail rapidly.

'What's got you so happy?' Maisy stared up at her happily.

Silly dog. 'Come on, let's get you some food.' She led Maisy down the hall.

It was already 4pm, and Kaitlyn slouched into the squeaky couch flicking through the channels on the old 2000 Sony TV. A piece of junk, that's what it was. She slouched more. 'There's nothing to watch on this thing,' she complained.

Mum was working her usual late nightshift. *She never has time for me.*

Kaitlyn sighed. 'What's the point in life?' she turned and asked Maisy. As if she could understand her, Maisy tilted her head confused.

Whatever.

Kaitlyn turned back to the useless television, then turned it off and chucked the remote aside. Then, as usual the familiar thoughts began to form in her head, the ones that always came, every day and every night.

I'm never good enough, nobody even cares about me. Tears threatened Kaitlyn as the dark thoughts became worse.

I should just make it easier for everyone.

Feeling overwhelmed, she stood and walked into the kitchen.

As she wiped a tear away with one hand, she poured a big glass of water with the other, opened the medicine cabinet and grabbed all the paracetamol she could find. She slid to the floor as tears streamed down her cheeks.

There were only two half-empty boxes. She lifted the two sleeves of tablets and popped them out into her hand. She took a big sip of water and, just as she was about to take the tablets, a vibration buzzed in her pocket.

She grabbed her phone. *Ugh, why call now?*

She groaned and answered the call without reading the contact. 'Who is it?' she said attempting to hide the wobble in her voice.

'Hey, It's Mum. Just wanted to check on you before the dinner rush.'

'Oh hey, Mum. Yeah, I'm fine...Just getting some water.' *Along with two dozen tablets.*

'Okay, good you're staying hydrated. There's a frozen pizza that you can cook for dinner.'

'Okay, thanks Mum. Bye.' She responded short and quick, about to hang up when her mum spoke again, 'Uh, honey, are you okay if I work a few extra hours tonight? Jem called in sick again and there's no available cover,' she asked nervously.

Typical! Of course she wasn't calling to 'just check on me'.

'Mmhm,' Kaitlyn mumbled.

'Hey, Kaitlyn.' Her mum paused. 'You know that I love you very much, sweetie. I know I haven't said it much lately. I don't know what I'd do without you.'

After a short silence Kaitlyn replied, 'Love you too. Um, have a good shift.'

'Thanks, hon, see you tomorrow.'

After ending the call, Kaitlyn smiled. *Mum hasn't said anything like that for months.*

She slowly got up from the cold tiles, wiped her tears with her forearm, and placed the tablets into a zip-lock bag.

Kaitlyn tossed and turned in her bed, frustrated that she couldn't sleep. She grabbed her phone from underneath her pillow.

12:03am. Ugh, fall asleep already!

The thoughts came back and continued throughout the night, causing Kaitlyn to stay awake.

Mum doesn't really love me. She was obviously lying to me. I was a mistake. Kaitlyn covered her ears as the thoughts continued, as if it would help.

Just get the pills and end this misery.

'No!' Kaitlyn cried out.

It shouldn't be like this. Why can't I control my mind!

She gave up. It was too hard. She threw off the covers and walked back to the kitchen, grabbed the pills from the cabinet and walked to the bathroom. She stared into the mirror. *There is no reason for me to live.*

She looked at the zip-lock bag, nodded and opened it, but her phone vibrated. *Ugh, what now!*

'Hello?' Kaitlyn asked with an annoyed tone.

'Hey Kaitlyn, it's Amber. You've been on my mind, are you okay?'

The bag dropped from her hand, pills spilling. 'Darn it,' she said to herself. *Why is Amber calling me? This is the second time I've been interrupted.*

'Amber? It's the middle of the night…' she responded, confused.

'I know. Sorry, did I wake you?' Amber said.

'No, no. I was already awake – glued to a book.' Was that convincing enough?

'Oh yeah, that always happens to me. So, I haven't seen you around much lately, what have you been up to? I've missed hanging out with you at school!' Amber chirped.

'Oh, yeah, I've been busy with a garden project.' Another lie.

'Ooh, fun! I could come over and help you out sometime, if you want.'

'I don't know, it's kind of a personal goal, you know. I want it to be me who does the work. But thanks, um, for offering.' Another lie.

'That's all good, I totally understand! Just thought I'd offer a hand,' Amber said.

'Thanks, though. Um…' *What does she want?*

'So, you're doing alright?' Amber asked again. 'I know the holidays can be a bit lonesome.'

Kaitlyn formed a lined frown. *What do I say?* 'Um, well yeah, you know, it's the holidays. Why would I not be…okay?' She picked at her nails as a tear streamed down her face. *Don't cry.* She sniffled loudly, covered her mouth. *No! why did I do that!*

'Kaitlyn...are you alright?' Amber asked, concerned.

'I'm...' she sniffled, 'I'm fine, Amber. I have a cold,' she lied, trying to use an amused tone.

'Kaitlyn, please don't hide from me. I want to help,' Amber begged.

'How do you know what I'm feeling? You have the perfect life, but my mum hates me and I'm just your charity case. It's okay, don't deny it,' Kaitlyn blurted, tears overtaking her. She struggled to breathe.

Ugh, I'm so stupid. Amber probably thinks that I need fixing because I'm one of the 'lost' like Christians call us. She doesn't care. Maybe she feels guilty.

'What? No! Kaitlyn, you're my friend. I care about you. Don't shut me out.' Amber said defensively. There was a silence for a moment. 'Kaitlyn, don't ever think that nobody cares. Your mum, she really loves you. Whenever I see her when she's working, she's always bragging to everyone about her smart and beautiful daughter,' Amber started. 'She is so proud of you. I know you may not think it, but she really does love you so much!'

Kaitlyn rubbed her nose with a sleeve as the crying continued.

'Kaitlyn, I know it might feel like the world is against you. I understand, I truly do. But you are so loved, and this world needs you! I need you and so does your mum.'

More silence.

'Please, Katy. Talk to me.'

Kaitlyn sniffled. She opened her mouth to speak but nothing came out.

'Katy..." Amber spoke quietly.

"I – I…' Kaitlyn stuttered. *Does Amber really care? Is she right? Does Mum really love me?* She sighed. 'I've attempted suicide two times today, but I kept getting interrupted.' She began to sob. 'Amber, I…I'm not okay.' *I need help.*

Six months later, Kaitlyn flopped onto her bed after coming home from Connect group. She scanned her journal entry from two weeks before. Wow. Her life had changed so much in the last few months.

> *Amber intervened just in time – God's timing. After revealing to her my attempts, she stayed on the phone with me until Mum came home, which showed how much she cared. The next day she told me about a counsellor that had really helped her when she was in a similar mindset. Surprising how Amber had felt the same way at some point. She hid it well.*
>
> *So, I've started seeing Mrs Janet on a weekly basis and she's helping me to talk about my feelings and taught me techniques to control my obsessive thoughts.*
>
> *On top of that, Amber has been bringing me to her church's girls Connect group, which is run by her older cousin, Sarah. All the girls are nice and welcoming. They've all shared about their own experiences. We have worship time and snacks, and then get into some devotions and prayer. It's very fun, and I feel my faith in God growing stronger. I've*

started coming to the Sunday services too. Anyway, it's late and I have school in the morning.

Kaitlyn smiled and yawned at the reminder – time for bed.

If anything in this story has raised issues for you, please call Lifeline on 131 114 (a 24-hour crisis service in Australia) or go to their website (www.lifeline.org.au) to learn more about their services.

Wonderfully Made!

Helena Stretton

'It's time!' the optician said, peering at my eyes through her latest high-tech machine. This was a regular eye check-up and my cataracts had developed further. An appointment with an eye surgeon was duly made. At that appointment I was given a folder full of information, including a spectacular coloured picture of the eye and details of the cataract operation. Surgery dates were given, three days apart for both eyes.

I recalled reading a similar but more detailed description in a less medical style years earlier, that left me in amazement at the structure and functioning of our eyes. I was able to locate it for a re-read:

> *'Who would believe,' asked Leonardo da Vinci, 'that so small a space could contain the images of all the universe...so great a wonder?'...*
>
> *Inside, a precision lens made of living tissue is slung with transparent protectors and kept in position by a clear liquid that renews itself constantly to nourish the cells and kill stray germs...*
>
> *The complexity of perceptual cells beggars the imagination. In humans, 127 million cells called rods and cones line up in rows as the 'seeing' elements that receive light and transmit messages to the brain. Rods, slender and graceful tentacles that reach out toward light, outnumber the*

> *bulbous cones 120 million to 7 million. These rod cells are so sensitive that the smallest measurable unit of light, one photon, can excite them; under optimum conditions, the human eye can detect a candle at a distance of fifteen miles...*
>
> *Our assortment of rods and cones lets us see objects at the end of our noses and also stars light years away.*[†]

I was again left in awe and mentioned this to the surgeon when we next met on the day of the first operation. 'We still don't know all there is to know about the eye,' he said, inferring such is the complexity and intricacy of its workings.

During the post-operation period with weeks of daily eye drops (a rigorous routine of three different kinds throughout each day), I happened to mention to a small group of friends I meet with weekly the wonders of the human eye, and how the beautiful description I'd read had inspired me! So much so, I added, that I wished my surgeon could read it too. Not that it would tell him anything he didn't already know, but the way it was written would underline the solemn and exquisite marvel that the eye really is. And in this way I would be paying tribute to the extraordinary work he does to repair such!

'Then show it to him at your next appointment!' the group said.

I immediately thought it could come across as inappropriate, a bit brash even, to take up his precious time with details he already

---

† Paul Brand and Philip Yancey, *In His Image*, Zondervan 1984, 2008.

knew. One then added, 'I once gave my surgeon some chocolates to express my gratitude to him. It was much appreciated. So just do it! We'll keep you accountable.' I sensed they would too!

When the follow-up appointment with my surgeon came, I arrived with chocolates and photocopied pages, attractively packaged. Then when it was time to leave I said that I had something for him. Taking the package, he exclaimed, 'A present?'

I expected him to receive it with thanks and put it aside to inspect later when less busy, for busy he was, as I noted each patient was taken to five different machines in three different rooms, and at times he seemed to have patients in all three! But he unpacked my gift, and started to read.

This gave me opportunity to explain it more, saying that it had enlightened me to the intricate marvels of the eye, and thus of his amazing skill and ability of the finest imaginable use of scalpel that he would have performed on my eyes. As a result he had set me up with excellent sight for the rest of my days!

'You have to have a very steady hand,' he said, his only words apart from a warm 'Thank you'!

I would always be so grateful to him and his team, I added, and that such has been available to me in this country when thousands of other people worldwide can only wish for it.

As I headed to the reception desk to pay my bill, fumbling in my handbag for my credit card as I did so, he went ahead and whispered to the receptionist before walking away. As I was about to hand her my card, she said, with a sideways shake of her head and half a smile, 'That's all for you today. You're good to go!'

I was too stunned for words and could only put my card back in my bag, deeply humbled by such unexpected generosity from one who was really a stranger. God's unmerited grace had been at work.

Elections can be Dangerous
Roslyn Bradshaw

'The kids aren't home. It's already 4 o'clock!' Norman's wife's voice trembled. 'What if they've been in an accident?'

Or worse, he thought. Without a phone, he felt helpless. He drove to the Bible college and rang the inter-mission school their teenage daughter and two sons attended daily. He tried to sound unconcerned as he enquired. The school knew nothing. Nobody else had phones.

He returned to their Javanese-style suburban home, praying, *Lord, keep them safe.*

Usually, the kids went to school in the mountains by early morning inter-city bus. It was an hour from the frenetic, diesel-infused bus station to their stop in peaceful Salatiga. An exhilarating, heart-stopping hour. Buses, cars, motorbikes and trucks pushed and shoved, vying for any skerrick of advantage.

'Did you see that bus in the ditch?'

'What about the oxcart that nearly got us in an accident?'

As evening approached, the trio came through the door laughing and chatting in the usual way. Both parents heaved a sigh of relief and calmly said, 'If you are going to be late, please ask someone to ring the college.'

When the Gulf War had broken out in 1990, the Foreign Affairs Department had suggested Australians leave Indonesia, fearing reprisals against foreigners. The family chose to stay, quietly teaching and preaching, stocking up on groceries, and avoiding hot spots. At election time, they took the same approach. They soon got used to rapid bursts of gunfire, as one party after another had crazy, roaring, street campaigns. Utes filled with hyped-up young men drove through crowded streets, megaphones screeching slogans, surrounded by hordes of revving motorbikes.

On shopping trips, the Australian boys were thrilled to see uniformed men brandishing submachine guns on every street corner.

'That's an AK-47!'

'Kalashnikov!'

'What about the Molotov cocktail!?'

Eventually, election fervour exploded. A local lad on a scooter died, run over by his own gun-toting faction. The danger level of the school run went up a notch. On the day before the vote, Norman decided that he needed to run the gauntlet of the winding road up to the school. His knuckles were white when he picked up the kids. *Get home NOW.*

The long, torturous drive home went peacefully enough until an election cavalcade came charging down the road, sweeping all before it like a monsoonal river. Motorbikes wove in and out, horns honking, bare-headed young enthusiasts shouting and waving flags. Norman's heart beat faster, sweat soaked his shirt. He slowed. Eyes darting about, looking for danger. Looking for a safe passage.

Suddenly there was smoke. Something landed in his lap. He tossed it back out the open window, smarting eyes scanning the melee. Rubbed his leg where he felt the heat. Smelt burnt cloth. Felt holes in his clothes. *Not a good place to stop. Keep driving. Don't draw attention. Get home.*

In Australia, prayer warriors sensed a need to ramp up their prayers, praying for safety and wisdom. Angels sped on assignment. The kids sat with eyes wide open, glued to the scene, and the dark sea of vehicles, bodies and smoke parted before them. Norman drove safely through and home without further incident. Unflappable.

Elections can be scary in Indonesia, but, he reflected, it *was* only a bundle of flaming straw, not a Molotov cocktail. Praise the Lord.

Playing Hands

Karen Curran

'That's middle C, Karen,' Mrs Farrington said, as she pointed to the middle of her piano, "followed by D, E, F, G, A, B, and then another C." She guided my fingers to one note after another. Cops and robbers with the Farrington boys had held my interest for a while, but, as always, the piano drew me like a magnet. I caressed the keys, and pressed one after another – some soft, some hard – pleased by the sounds they made. My neighbour pulled out a songbook and explained how to read notes. Before long I could play 'Mary Had a Little Lamb,' and 'Row, Row, Row Your Boat'. If my fingers had had mouths, they would have all been smiling. My face certainly was. I had no particular passion for the familiar songs I was playing, but those sounds ringing from the piano resonated through every molecule in my body and set my spirit soaring.

I was seven when my parents finally bought a piano. We had moved a few months before, far away from the Farrington home, and I had discovered that I did not like life without that wonderful instrument.

'Karen's hands are too small,' the neighbourhood piano teacher said, as I stretched my fingers as far as they could go. 'She needs to be able to reach an octave before I can take her as a student.' My heart sank.

At home, I played the few songs I knew over and over, and strained to reach those eight notes. After months of listening to me beg and cry, Mother took me back to the teacher, who finally agreed to take me on. My sister might as well have quit her lessons because I laid claim to the piano then, playing for hours every day.

My fingers never tired of the chance to make music. Beautiful, glorious music.

I continued to play, year after year, accompanying choirs and soloists and mastering increasingly difficult music: Beethoven, Rachmaninoff, Gershwin. A Bachelor of Arts degree in Music stood at the top of my list as I prepared to go to college.

The summer of my seventeenth year, just after high school graduation, an unexpected thing happened. It started with pain in my right knee, but quickly spread throughout my body. I lay in bed looking at the swollen finger joint over which my size three ring would no longer fit.

'Do you think I'll ever play the piano again?' I asked my mother.

'Of course you will, Karen, she said, with a brave smile. I learned later that she went to the next room and cried.

A specialist diagnosed rheumatoid arthritis and prescribed medication. By the time I left for college the inflammation was under control, the swelling diminished. My joints, however, were weak and fragile. No physical education classes for me. I had to stop and rest in each stairwell, simply climbing the three flights to my dorm room. Managing the hills on the mountain campus was hard enough; hours of piano practice were out of the question.

I settled on business classes and found some enjoyment typing and adding columns of numbers. Those activities made sense and seemed useful; they certainly kept my hands busy. Typing and using a calculator were reminiscent of playing a piano, though without the lovely sounds.

Two years after graduating in accounting, and six years after getting sick, the disease simply went away. In remission, the doctor said, no explanation given.

My short-lived affliction changed the course of my life. Or rather, I should say, God changed it. I considered myself a piano player. He saw me, instead, not as the player, but as the instrument itself – his instrument – a part of his grand orchestra of life. He has guided me through careers in tax accounting, retail sales, and church music. Most importantly, he has walked alongside me as my husband and I parented two children.

I still love to play, the beautiful sounds of the piano reverberating through the house like prayers. But I have become so much more than what I aimed to be. God has shown that there is no limit to what he can do, not only when my hands play for him, but when I become the very instrument on which God plays his melodies of life.

At Home in Lilliput

Paula Vince

Once I took my daughter and youngest son into the city to visit the museum on his birthday. We discovered school students getting hands-on workshops from a group of scientists who each had a small aquarium full of dirt. We happened to walk in at the very end of a session. As the school class filed out, one of the presenters seemed to be at a loose end. He smiled and beckoned us over to his table.

'Would you like to see something cool? Use this spoon to sprinkle some dirt from the tank onto my microscope slide. You go first, young man, and then your sister,' he said. 'I'll show you exactly what you've picked up.'

With a sheepish grin, my son scooped a brown clod from the mound onto the glass slide. Our friendly guide homed in on it with his lens and pointed to a computer screen.

'What you've found here is the jawbone of a praying mantis. See its sharp angle? They eat lots of other tiny insects. And next to it is a claw from a finch's foot. Check out the detail of the scaly pattern. No two are exactly alike.' He turned to my daughter. 'Now it's your turn.'

She randomly dug into another section of the aquarium and came up with an offering that appeared identical to her brother's.

'Okay, there's the knee joint of a grasshopper. See how it looks a bit like a knob in a socket? That's the part that would have helped him spring. It appears sinewy beneath the screen because it's so strong. It could propel him several feet with one bound. And right here is a marsupial's toenail. There's the sharp point. Somehow he ripped it right off as he was hopping.'

We had this interesting man all to ourselves for the next half hour. As my two kids took turns to shake more dirt onto the microscope slides, he continued to reveal a Lilliputian world invisible to the naked eye. Filmy gnat's wings and shafted dandelion spores, broken seed husks from which sprouts had thrust themselves, even occasional luminous fish scales. All from his unassuming glass container full of homogenous looking dirt.

Approaching chatter from another school group grew louder, so he shook our hands and thanked the kids for humouring him. The pleasure was all ours. We walked along the riverbank back to our car with the surreal suspicion that we might be stomping on a teeming ecosystem we knew nothing about.

'I could have talked with him all day,' my son said, as he buckled up his seatbelt.

'Yeah, me too.'

Our fascinating encounter with the generous stranger triggered an interest in the natural world that remained strong for several months. My daughter bought a good quality camera with money she'd earned from her part-time job. She enjoyed zooming in close to her subjects and even that opened a world of finer detail we'd previously brushed past.

The wing of a moth near the bathroom light resembled the shaggy flank of Sesame Street's Mr Snuffleupagus. Common weed petals were seen to have perfect scalloped edges, as if cut intentionally by tiny pinking shears. The compound eyes of a resting blowfly gleamed like the domed roof of the Adelaide Arcade. And our guinea pig's teeth resembled fierce, curved sabres. The kids were delighted, and their new habit of probing deeper added awe and wonder to my life too.

Yet I couldn't deny a niggling sense of guilt for never stopping to notice all this before. The world was bursting at its seams with wonder to which I'd been essentially oblivious. I questioned whether my blindness was completely my fault, since God made these teeming minutiae microscopic. Why would he bother to fill our planet with such intricate detail for the benefit of unmindful barbarians like myself, who rarely pause to take it in? What was the point of making an incredibly detailed world, if few people cared or realised? I felt like a crass buffalo wallowing in a hothouse flower garden. It wasn't a pleasant feeling.

The kids didn't share my sense of remorse. They were young enough not to feel as if they had wasted decades with their eyes closed.

One afternoon my perspective flipped right over. As I drove along with the car radio on, a cosmonaut was being interviewed on a talkback channel. He described how he'd looked forward to seeing Mount Everest from up in space yet found it very hard to discern the landmark when he got there. From a hundred kilometres above the earth's surface, the mighty Everest simply blended in with the rest of the earth's crust. And as for other great mountains, in his opinion they might as well have been pimples or pencil dots.

That gave me something new to ponder. I'd spent the last several weeks picturing myself as a giant who walked rough shod over precious natural treasures. However, from a broad enough celestial perspective, I realised I am miniscule myself, no less than the plankton, fleas and pygmy mushrooms that had so recently caught my attention. I moved on from the question, 'Why does God bother to embellish such tiny things which hardly ever make it onto most people's radars?' Instead, I decided, 'I don't know why he does it, but I sure am grateful these miniature marvels are infused and decorated with such painstaking detail, since I am one of them.'

One of my favourite novels is *Rilla of Ingleside*, featuring the daughter of Anne of Green Gables. Rilla Blythe and her family live during World War One, a time period in which heartache is inevitable. Rilla's three brothers and the boy she loves all join the Canadian army and fight in the trenches, where Walter, her favourite brother, is killed.

Rilla's teacher, Gertrude Oliver, worn down by grief, has a desperate question for the local minister. 'We think very lightly, Mr Meredith, of a calamity which destroys an anthill and half its inhabitants. Does the Power that runs the universe think *us* of more importance than we think the ants?'

The wise man is worried sick over the plight of his own soldier sons. Yet he has the confidence to tell her, 'You forget that an infinite power must be infinitely little as well as infinitely great. We are neither. Therefore, there are things too little as well as too great for us to comprehend. To the Infinitely Little, an ant is of as much importance as a mastodon'.[†]

His words always thrill me. The scope of all that we had seen, first through the powerful museum microscope and secondly through our own zoom camera lens suggests that we can depend on them. Our galaxy with its enormous planets and black holes is unimaginably vast, but the atoms, cells and mitochondria which form our own hands and feet are equally mind-blowingly petite. Even if our earth is comparatively as tiny as Lilliput, it doesn't matter. It's comforting to reflect that the Infinitely Little has got us covered.

† LM Montgomery, *Rilla of Ingleside*, Angus & Robertson, 1980.

Not Alone

Rebekah Matson

I sat on the edge of my son's hospital bed. The first time alone in days. He had gone to the Starlight Room (a room with games and activities for sick children and their families) for a little while and I had decided to stay back. My mind was reeling. My breath was hard to catch. My chest tightened. Tears started to escape, slowly at first, then with quickening pace that no amount of wiping could stop. I could no longer control it and began to 'ugly cry' as my children call it. The grief, of not only the last few days but also the déjà vu of experiencing chronic illness with another one of my children, had overcome me.

At least this time they had answers.

Still, all I could hear, as if stuck on repeat, were the doctors' words: 'life-threatening' and 'life-long'.

Overlapping those phrases, I heard replays of an old woman from our church speaking to me vehemently a few weeks earlier, saying one of my children would die. And in this moment, I felt she might be right. At the time she had said it, I had rebuked her: 'How dare you speak that over my children's lives!' Now I wasn't so sure.

I wasn't feeling strong. I grappled with the old woman's words that filled me with foreboding, a barb into my heart that made me question myself. Had I somehow brought this on my child? Was I, or my faith, a fake? The thoughts pressed on. Crushing me. Despair creeping in, and seeping out in a wail I could hear coming out of my body. Yet I was unable to stop it, like I had become detached, watching on. The more I tried to quiet myself, the louder I felt I became.

The crescendo of despair engulfing me came to a sudden halt as I briefly opened my eyes in my slumped over mess and saw two feet. I stopped the cry and tried, unsuccessfully at first, to steady my breathing, looked up and realised it was a friend. I don't know how long he had been standing there. Dave had been a friend of our family for years. He has an amazing ability, despite his commanding physical presence, to enter a room unnoticed.

I was embarrassed for him to see me like this. But he seemed unfazed.

'I was coming to see if you were alright, but I suppose that is unnecessary.'

I meekly nodded whilst still feeling the after effects of the rapid breathing from my meltdown just moments before.

'Here, I brought you this,' he said, passing me a coffee and a muffin.

I thanked him and wiped away the tears that were still escaping.

He brought out a pack of cards. '500?'

I couldn't think straight and was unsure if I could offer any competition but I got what he was doing and so I agreed.

My first few hands I don't even really remember, except he had to keep reminding me what card to play. Slowly my brain re-entered the present and I could focus and give him a run, even if he still won. My son arrived back from his play time at the Starlight Room, oblivious to what had transpired in the room in his absence. He was buzzing about receiving a new Lego set and a brown balloon animal gone wrong that they named, much to my 11-year-old son's delight, 'Poo on a stick'. I had calmed down enough that I think Dave felt safe to leave me, and so after a quick chat with my son he left.

We settled in for the evening routine we'd become accustomed to since our arrival at the hospital. We'd pick a movie, start watching, be interrupted by the nurses taking their observations and giving him his medicine. They would small-talk and we would tell them what was happening with the movie and then after they finally left, we would continue watching.

This night, the nurses had just left and we were settling in to watch the movie again. *Finding Dory* was our movie of choice for the night. Having watched it before, my mind began to wander. Thoughts I was having earlier began to rise again. I didn't want my son to see me like I had been earlier and add to what he was facing. I quickly let out a 'help, Jesus' under my breath, and then deliberately focused on the movie, putting on an aloof demeanour for my son. Dory's personality and the clever one-liners managed to help quell the gloom for a moment; I even laughed a few times, which had a healing feeling of its own.

The door to our room opened, and since it was after visiting hours, I thought the nurses had forgotten something. Instead, in walked the migrant mother of some of the children that had come to our church children's programs. She said she had heard my son was sick and felt she was to come and pray. She had worked a long shift that day and was very tired, so was planning on leaving it until tomorrow, but had a nagging feeling it was important that she came tonight.

'Would it be alright if I pray?' she asked.

'That would be good', my son answered before I could reply.

She smiled, knelt on the hospital floor beside my son's bed with her hands raised to the ceiling.

'Thank you, Lord, for this young man's life,' she began, and then startled me by saying unexpectedly, "I break off any curse that has been declared over this family's life! The enemy has intended harm, but we know you, Lord. Turn it for good. I declare your goodness over this young man, in Jesus' name!"

She had no idea what I had been grappling with, or what that old lady had spoken that had gotten inside my head, but she spoke straight to it!

I cannot remember anything else of what she said that night, but I remember seeing my son, eyes closed, tears rolling down his cheeks. He didn't know about the curse. The prayer and the atmosphere in the room was touching him. I had closed my eyes and remember feeling so warm, like someone had put a bonfire in the room. I felt peace penetrate my soul and dislodge the despair.

My new friend finished her prayer with a short song in her language, stood, hugged my son and me, and left. I never saw her again as she moved interstate soon after this. I never got to tell her how much she helped me through her simple obedience and powerful prayer.

Both visitors that day, though their methods completely differed, were answers to prayers I couldn't even speak. I realise sometimes our prayers aren't answered by miraculously being healed or our troubles melting away. Mostly it's by other humans being obedient to a prompting to enter an uncomfortable space and be present. My sons may not be instantaneously healed, and we walk the somewhat painful journey of chronic illness, but not in despair. Nights when I awake and I feel that fear and grief threaten

Not Alone

to overwhelm me, I remind myself we are not alone, and that gives me hope.

The Minute
Jie Ni

An overcast sky.
   Railway station.
   A city in Australia.
   Monday.
   Big crowds.

She was the first one in the queue validating tickets. As soon as the ticket machine gave a beeping sound, she pushed hard on the exit gate and went straight to the escalator around the corner. She is from China and normally enjoys crowds; somehow the more the merrier, as it makes her feel at home.

But not today. In fact, the minute she stepped up a few levels on the escalator, hoping to quickly get out of the busy station, something in her sank, like the cloud in the sky. This feeling of heaviness was not welcome, but the minute she tried to push it away, she heard a voice screaming in her head, 'Why does that woman keep bothering me!'

'That woman!' The minute these two words popped out, a shock came upon her. How could she address her mum like that? Even in her wildest thoughts, she would never call her 'that woman', because in the Chinese culture that was utterly disrespectful. Also, for all these years she has been trying her very best to be a good Christian. After all, a good Christian is able to always smile, always hold it all together, and always ready to forgive others when being wronged, she thought.

But now it looked like she has failed and lost it all. A huge sense of guilt swamped her; at the same time, confusion started to arise because the minute she said what was on her mind, she could feel a big relief, like a sack of stone off her shoulder immediately. Finally, she was true to her feelings and could express it: she really could not handle anymore of her mother's nagging.

Being caught in between these mixed emotions, she was not sure where to go, mentally.

The minute she felt stuck, another voice landed in her ears, but this time it was a gentle but firm one, '"That woman", as you just called her, is my precious daughter! I love her deeply!'

If there had been a pillow on the floor, the minute she heard this voice, she would have knelt down and begged for mercy, his mercy. And she did, in her heart, with an invisible pillow; she said sorry to God and asked for his forgiveness. 'Yes, God, my mum is your precious daughter and I am very sorry that I was unkind to her!'

Two years later.
 China.
 A city in the south.
 Home.
 One day after lunch.

'I warned you many times not to give up your lecturing job at the university to go into ministry, but you just would not listen… Now you have to bear the consequence, see how difficult you have made life for yourself! I urge you to…' Mum sighed, while collecting the dishes on the table.

Oh, not again. Over the last few years, this nagging has been always there in her brain, even when she and Mum were thousands of miles apart, one in China and one in Australia; and it had been so distressing that she was needing to seek counselling help in Australia.

This time when she came home to visit family, to her astonishment, Mum had kept silent for a good few days and did not mention a thing in regards to her choice, and she was then able to start to feel peaceful with Mum around. But it seems Mum's streams of anxiety have now merged into rivers and even oceans and all the words that have been saved are suddenly all poured out.

The minute the nagging flooded into her ears, all these years of accumulated stress in her seemed not to be able to be bottled up anymore. Like a volcano, it erupted. Clenching her teeth, her whole body started trembling; her hands started to grip tightly the edge of the lunch table. But the physical body reaction was just the tip of the iceberg; inside, there was even more turmoil.

'Mum, why can't you understand? I love God and can give up anything to serve him.' She almost shouted. She felt she had the best position in this long unresolved conflict. After all, surely she was right because she wanted to serve God!

She wanted to cry and use her tears to tell the whole world how unfairly she had been treated and tell Mum that Mum was wrong; but the minute the tears formed, to her surprise, she heard a whimpering sound. Looking up, she saw tears dripping down her mother's face.

Mum never cried, not even when seeing her off at the airport. Dad had been the one crying, feeling sad each time about his daughter leaving home.

'But hold on! Am I not the one who should be sobbing after all the years of being pressured by her?' The complaints turned to their maximum volume in her head, every cell in her wanted to jump out and protest, as a victim is supposed to do, until the minute…

A voice flowed in, again, gently, 'Pray, step out of yourself, go and apologise to your mum!'

The minute she heard this voice, her tight-rolled fingers loosened, and with it, something tight in her chest was released. Her arms relaxed and moved away from the edge of the table and formed a cross shape. She prayed. 'God, help me!'

The minute that was said, there came an unexplainable strength in her, lifting her up from the chair. She went up to Mum.

'I am so sorry, Mum!'

The words could still be heard clearly, even though she was so clumsy in the way she said it. These few words were new and foreign to her; for over forty years she had never said such a thing. (Of course, it's not that she never felt sorry to Mum, but in her culture, when one person did something wrong, this person will do something to compensate the other persons' loss, instead of using a verbal apology.) So really, on that day, her lips and teeth were trying hard for the very first time to form the articulation of the syllables.

But the minute that was said, magic appeared; Mum's face lit up, and her tone of voice softened. For the first time in her life, she felt close to Mum. All these years of stress dissolved and melted, the minute that apology from the heart was spelled out.

Mum looked at her with a look she had never seen before and will never forget; she followed her mum to Mum's bedroom. Sitting beside Mum on a bamboo mat, she felt like a baby again. She then opened herself up and was completely vulnerable. For the first time in her life, the mum and daughter had a heart to heart conversation, sweet like honey.

Two months later.
 Over the phone. She is back in Australia, and talking to Mum in China.
 'No, that cannot be true, Mum!' Her voice rose.
 'But it is!' Mum's voice was even louder on the other side of the phone.
 The minute her dad heard the volume go up, feeling anxious about a quarrel approaching, he grabbed the phone from Mum. 'Please do not argue, it's time for you both to sleep.'
 'Oh, come on, it's only 8pm!' Mum and daughter said together without looking at each other. Sensing the man's uncertainty, they assured him, 'Sorry, we are a bit loud; don't worry, we are good! Thanks to God!'
 And the minute that was said, she noticed her notebook on the table; it was filled with notes from listening to Mum advising on how to pastorally care for younger women. She felt supported and loved.
 Indeed, the love between them has never been stronger, because God's divine intervention changed everything and restored their relationship. In Christ, they could be true to themselves and to each other. In recent years, Mum even learnt how to use emojis on her phone and would send her greetings each morning, calling her, 'my most precious treasure!' and she to Mum, 'my honey Mum!'
 The 'minute' we are true to ourselves and to each other, and the minute we bow to God, the outcome of our choice is completely different, almost instantly.

Becoming Unmasked
Teri Kempe

The boss where I volunteer mentioned speaking to an American lady who now lives in Victoria. She thought we would have much in common and suggested I call her.

It was one of those calls where you make immediate connections. We found so many things we had in common. She was active in prison ministry, as I was. She also had a love for Israel. But her stunning revelation was that she had been transformed by an encounter with Jesus and moved to Australia after coming out of a secret drug addiction. She wrote about it in a memoir called *Unmasked*.

'That's amazing,' I responded. 'I wrote a book during the Covid pandemic, called *Living Unmasked*.'

We agreed to exchange books and keep in touch.

Next day I went to the post office. On the way I stopped at the restroom. I placed the copy of *Living Unmasked* on the ledge while I washed my hands. I noticed a young lady looking intently at my book.

'Excuse me. Is that a good book?'

'Of course, I wrote it,' I laughed.

'Oh, that's amazing. May I take a look?'

She picked up the book and read the back blurb. She was shaking her head, obviously perplexed.

'I wrote it during the pandemic lockdowns,' I said, 'because it seemed to me God was giving us a second chance. Although we had to wear a surgical mask all the time, in fact God was unmasking us. Everything we thought gave us our identity was actually taken away. We couldn't do all the things we loved, like visiting family, going to church, the footy or the pub. Then I started looking at the Bible and found there were many people he unmasked: Adam and Eve, King Saul, King David, Peter – the list goes on.'

'That's amazing!' she said. 'Last night I had a dream in which God spoke to me very clearly. He said, "Take off your mask. Stop pretending! Be yourself!" I didn't really understand it but meeting you here is extraordinary. I think we were meant to meet.'

This young lady came from Melbourne. She was only in Sydney for a day and on her way to a business meeting. We were both stunned by the encounter, exchanged details and agreed to keep in touch.

Beauty Scars

Anastasia Korkodyllos

There are certain moments in life where time seems like it has stopped.

You know, completely, suddenly stood still.

Those moments…those are the ones that change a person.

Those moments cannot be gotten over. Only gotten through.

Those moments stay…as a part of you.

But those moments don't have to be your whole moment forever.

I know that my story isn't the only story. There are so many. I think it is important to share our stories, because you just never know who needs to hear your story and who you can encourage or uplift or challenge through sharing it.

I had a moment. A moment I chose to live in for six years. But first an overview:

I had a great childhood, grew up in a Christian home, gave my heart to Christ at eighteen, got married at twenty-one, also got diagnosed with a malignant melanoma in the year I got married, but God still wanted me here.

My mum (who was not just my ma, she was my everything) got diagnosed with bowel cancer, went through surgery, chemo and radiotherapy. She said, with a smile, 'God's got me, let's do what we have to and the rest I'll leave in his hands.' I remember her making jokes about how she never had to worry about getting constipated anymore, as she now was living with a colostomy bag. People wouldn't know what to say to that, and she would laugh so they wouldn't feel awkward but also because she genuinely thought it was so funny.

When I was pregnant with my first child, I ended up having to have a caesarean, so Mum flew over from interstate to stay and help me for seven weeks. She then told me that her cancer was back and was worse this time. Doctors said it was terminal and gave her one year to live, at best. I was in shock. Hot tears streamed down my face. To me, this news was life-altering. My thoughts were, 'My everything is going to be taken away from me. How can I live without my everything?!' That's what she was to me.

Against doctor's predictions, Mum passed the one year mark. I fell pregnant with my second baby.

Mum had booked her flight to come stay and help me again. She had gotten worse health-wise but she was determined to be there for us. She stayed and helped for seven weeks.

Then. The text. She said she couldn't call. In the text she wrote that the cancer was spreading now and that doctors said she didn't have long left. Her wishes were for me to fly over with the kids to be there together with her in whatever weeks she had left. I was reluctant as I didn't want to be a burden to her with a toddler and a newborn baby. My husband told me I'd regret it if I didn't go. So I packed my bags and flew over with the kids.

The moment I entered my parents' home, I almost collapsed in disbelief at how quickly my mother had deteriorated. I remember her saying, 'Don't worry, I'm not dead'. That was Mum, always making hard situations into light-hearted moments.

The next two-and-a-half months were ones of helplessness and heartbreak but also reliance on God's strength and thankfulness that I got to have this special time with her.

God took her home on the 12th December 2009. I stayed to help my dad and my brother as much as I could to settle in with now having to live our lives without Mum.

I flew back home in February, back to reality. A reality I didn't want to face or deal with. I was not ready to live a life without my 'everything'. I remember I'd call Mum's mobile, in tears because I had had a hard day with the kids, sleep-deprived or wanting her advice, her prayers, or to just hear her voice that would always calm me…and then the thought, 'Oh…Mum's not there anymore'.

It took two years for it to sink into my brain that Mum was physically not on this earth anymore.

I was determined I didn't need anyone's help or pity or sympathy. So I shut everyone out of my life as best as I could. I also chose to shut God out too. If I couldn't have my 'everything' (Mum) then I didn't want anything.

I was in a valley. A deep, dark, lonely valley. I was living in *that* moment. For six years. God kept pursuing me. My marriage started falling apart. My relationship with God was put on hold. I felt so far from everyone. I felt so alone. So lost. Yet God kept pursuing me. I had a few people I knew that were fervently praying for me, that kept sending me verses from God's Word. I was numb. For a really long time.

Then God got my attention well and truly. I felt such a spiritual battle going on, I could physically feel the pressure being pushed in all around me. I was so scared. One evening, my youngest son was very unsettled. I knew something was up spiritually. I called the pastor who had married my husband and me and asked him to come and pray for us. He did, and he asked us if we were going anywhere to a Christian congregation. I said, 'No, not for many years'. He suggested somewhere to go.

So the next day we went. I remember saying to God: 'God, if you really want me back, if you truly do care about me, get this congregation to sing a Keith Green song. I'll know for sure then.' I didn't say a word to anyone. We sat there, heard the message that was being shared (which, by the way, hit that spot in my heart) but I still thought to myself, 'Ah well, no Keith Green song.'

And then as the pastor was finishing up, he said, 'I would like for us to close with a song that was written by a dear old friend of mine who isn't here anymore – Keith Green.'

I laughed. I had this big beaming smile on my face. My husband looked at me weirdly. I knew God was listening. He never stopped listening. He cared. About *all* the details.

I surrendered my all to him. I got unstuck from that moment.

He showed me a vision of myself in a deep, dark valley. It was so deep and dark that when I looked up I couldn't see any light. I saw his arm and hand stretched out, waiting for me to get up and take his hand. He said to me, 'I never intended for you to stay here for six years, but I waited for you, I stayed with you, I never left you.' And then I saw myself getting up and holding his hand and him leading me out of this deep dark valley. Then he said, 'Now that you have chosen to hold onto me again and follow me, come walk with me,' and he took me to the top, where there was fresh air and light and we walked forward together.

Beauty Scars

    Grief is a big thing. To feel the absence of someone is like there is a forever-missing puzzle piece…Truth is, there will always be a scar left behind, but once it been healed it becomes a story you can share…to give someone else hope who has not yet found hope.

    That is the beauty of a scar.

    Don't hide your scar.

    Share your scar story.

Plant a Seed
Dienece Darling

One April morning a few years ago, I was scrolling through Facebook Memories when I spotted an old post from a friend. 'All those that know (name removed) please pray. She has gone to hospital with heavy bleeding 1 week after giving birth and the doctors and nurses can't stop it. That's all I know for now.'

Even five years later, I could still feel the pressure of the moment, the fear crowding in. Fear not just for my friend but from personal experience. I'd haemorrhaged just after my first son was born. People would talk with me about having another kid, but all I could picture was the blood covering the floor.

I'd known something was wrong just after the birth, but I hadn't paid much heed to the chatter from the end of the bed. My obstetrician even asked the newbie if she'd 'like to have a go at this for practice.' So whatever they were doing couldn't be too serious, right? I'd preferred to focus on my newborn son.

When they finished and told me to shower, the blood stretched from the foot of the hospital bed into a puddle that took up most of the large, open space I'd paced while in labour. It was quite a shock to realise what the doctor had been nattering about. She said I only lost the bare minimum of blood to qualify for a haemorrhage, but to my mind I never wanted to learn how much worse it could be. And the doctor said I'd most likely haemorrhage again if I had another child. One baby was all it was going to be for me.

Yet a few weeks after my friend's ambulance ride to hospital and subsequent emergency surgery, she was posting on Facebook how annoyed she was people kept assuming she wouldn't have any more kids, because childbearing was a woman's place in life. Despite not agreeing with her conclusion, the sentiment behind her post planted a seed of doubt in my mind. If a woman who had experienced something far more traumatic could put it all aside to have another child, perhaps my fears weren't grounded.

I didn't give it much thought before pushing the doubt aside, but there that seed sat deep in my mind. Niggling, pushing, and growing little by little until the doubt sprouted and took weak root. Several years passed until that seed grew into a tree of change. I found the courage to trust God and have another child.

I couldn't tell my friend. She had unfriended me on Facebook sometime after her post about not fearing childbirth. I didn't notice at first, then I began to wonder why I hadn't seen posts from her. Upon investigation, I discovered we weren't friends anymore. Some people disparage 'so-called' Facebook friends, but if they'd seen my bleeding heart that moment, they'd have known virtual friends can be so very real.

Had I said something unintentionally offensive? I was pretty sure I'd kept all my negative thoughts about childbearing being 'a woman's place in life' to myself. Or had I? Oh, I hoped I hadn't allowed my fear to spill out into a nasty comment! All the animosity I'd first felt had faded away during the ensuing weeks. The seed of doubt she'd planted was still only a tender sprout, but it was already changing me.

I was pretty sure I hadn't said anything directly to her. But maybe that was the problem. I didn't interact with her posts much. Perhaps she'd culled me for that when whittling down her Facebook friends. Had I, horror of all horrors, missed one of those 'My true friends will…' posts? I hated those posts! Or, perhaps, she was just feeling stretched too thin trying to keep up with so many friends now a newborn was on hand. It could even be because she had moved overseas, and we never saw each other in person anymore.

What if it was a matter of privacy? But that would mean I wasn't on her chosen list of safe friends. That certainly didn't make me feel better.

No matter the excuse I imagined, nothing soothed my battered heart. Even five years later, seeing that Facebook memory stirred up the pain of our lost friendship as fresh as the moment I'd discovered her gone. This time I didn't make up a list of excuses to attempt to make myself feel better. I took a journey through time to evaluate myself as a friend.

I had never told my friend what she meant to me. Perhaps it was a little bit because she was the popular girl, and guilt ate away at me over how much I craved being friends with a popular girl. But she was more than that to me. She was just plain fun to be around, and I'd never told her so.

Now that I'd lost her friendship, I couldn't even tell her how much she'd changed my life. Not just through all the fun times we'd had together, but because my second child might never have been born if she hadn't planted that seed of doubt after her emergency surgery. It's odd how something so small as a few words on a fleeting Facebook post could produce something so wonderful. But there you go, and I couldn't even tell her because I'd lost my friend from my own cowardice, my own preoccupation with myself, my own guilt over being friends with a popular girl. I had destroyed my friendship.

I didn't limit myself to that one friend. I dug deep into all my relationships. How many people had I decided weren't my friends anymore? How many people had I casually unfriended? Sometimes we just don't realise how important we were to some people because they didn't have the courage to tell us, and we lacked the insight to notice.

My introspection showed I was not always a good friend, virtual or otherwise. Oh, I was happy to catch up with people, but I never took time to chase up my friends, see how they were, make time or put in effort for them. I'd be silent when I lacked the 'right' words to respond to a tough situation. I was the casual, when-it's-convenient friend.

I didn't want to be that anymore. I wanted to be the friend who put other people before me even if it wasn't convenient or when I had no idea what to say. To remember friendship takes at least two people. To be the one that considered the other person might value my friendship more than I do theirs. Knowing that not everyone will, of course, but just to be aware of the possibility because that was me once. To never again discount a virtual friend or treat them cavalierly.

I chose to act, to be the change I wanted. I found the courage to reach out to my old friend. Yes, my stomach twisted while hitting the send button on my message, but it resulted in a quickly rekindled friendship. It did my heart good to read the excited words and obvious joy in her reply. Turns out she had no idea how we'd lost touch and blamed the computer for unfriending us. It was good to know that however the loss of our friendship had happened, it hadn't been intentional on her part. That she was excited to be connected again.

That gave me the courage to reach out to another friend, one I had begun to realise I might have hurt. My stomach turned sour, and I cried for days with fear over what the outcome of that message might be. I'm glad I did it though, even if the result wasn't as happy as with my first friend. It was good for me to try to make amends, to take responsibility for poor decisions in the past.

I think I'm a much better friend now, and my life has been richly blessed by my second child. Yes, I haemorrhaged again when he was born, but God pulled us through. I hope that one day I might be able to plant a seed for someone else that will grow into something as beautiful as the seed my friend planted for me.

The Hand of God

Hazel Barker

My mother always believed in the power of prayer. The following incident, in particular, brought the fact home to me. Japan had occupied Burma in 1941. When Britain commenced retaking Burma in 1944, we took refuge in a village not far from the city of Mandalay, to escape the bombing.

We had been living under Japanese occupation for four years by then. We moved into a hut, and Mum and my little sister, Rose, remained indoors for fear of the Japanese while my father and two brothers, Rupert and Bertie, explored the jungle that surrounded us. Food was scarce, and we suffered from diarrhoea and beri-beri.

Perhaps because Rupert had wandered into the jungle and mosquito-infested swamps so frequently, he contracted malaria. For days he lay shivering in bed, a blanket pulled over his head even on the hottest days, because it is imperative for a patient with malaria to rest.

When he had perspired, the fever would disappear, leaving him weak and listless. Within a short time, the cycle would repeat itself, completely sapping his strength.

We had long run out of quinine. Dad called in a herbalist who prescribed neem tea and ordered Rupert to remain in bed.

Neem trees grew in profusion at the village. We picked the leaves and Mum boiled them as instructed. Rupert followed the herbalist's advice and drank cups of the herbal infusion without complaining. The bitter concoction broke his fever until the cycle recommenced within a few weeks.

By the end of 1944, it seemed death was about to place its hand on Rupert's shoulder and claim him. All our prayers seemed in vain.

By early 1945, British and Indian forces had fought their way back through northern Burma from India to the west, via the Ledo Road. From China to the east, American and Chinese forces entered Burma via the Stilwell Road. By March 1945, Allied troops were finally at the gates of Mandalay. One evening as the sun sank beneath the horizon and spread a dark mantle over the village, the sound of shells and the roar of trucks broke the stillness of the night. Convoys, like one continuous caterpillar, humped up and down the Mandalay-Maymyo Road, trucking Japanese re-enforcements to the northern frontline and returning with casualties to hospitals in Mandalay.

One night I heard explosions just over the hill. A rush of blood to my head caused a little light-headedness, and my heart hammered with the pounding of guns.

Day by day the thunder of twenty-pounders grew closer and louder. Allied forces crossed the river just south of Mandalay and, cutting off all road access to the city, they commenced a barrage of shelling. Shells roared and trucks rolled past on the Mandalay-Maymyo Road, behind which lay our village. Yet still village life carried on with its never-ending monotony.

My parents lived in fear of being trapped between the British and Japanese forces.

February slid into the hot days of March. One sweltering day, Rupert lay in bed shivering with malaria, a blanket covering his head. Weak and famished, Mum sat praying beside him. Dad was out. I and my siblings, Bertie and Rose, paced listlessly beneath the hut, which was built on stilts in case of flooding during the monsoon rains. Bertie gazed into the distance, his head to one side, as though he was trying to listen.

An uplifting sound echoed across the plains. We had heard it every New Year's Day in those wonderful days in Rangoon before the war. The skirl of bagpipes stirred the very core of my soul. Even now, I can shut my eyes and call to mind that glorious day. My pulse raced, but by the way my sister tightened her grip on my hand, I knew she was afraid. The sound was strange to her ears.

'It's the British!' Bertie streaked off, swift as an arrow, in the direction of the main road.

'Come on, Rose.' I held her hand and raced after him.

We rushed towards the call of the bagpipes, drawn like pieces of metal to a magnet. Bertie followed the haunting sound, cutting across fields, heedless of village dogs baying in competition with the music. Fields gave way to bushes, and soon we came to a row of trees lining the Mandalay-Maymyo Road. Kilt-clad Scots, replete with bagpipes and kettledrums, were followed by a large contingent of British soldiers marching four abreast. Magnificent in full uniform, they left no doubt they were the victors.

The whole village appeared to have turned out, standing on either side of the road. They gaped at the soldiers. Bertie found a place for us in front to watch the march. An exhilarating thrill ran up my spine. We stood in breathless silence while the stirring sound of martial music filled the valley and resounded over the plains. I gazed through a film of tears. *Did these smart soldiers trudge out of Burma, weary and footsore, when Japanese troops invaded Burma?* To my childish eyes, every soldier was a hero.

After a fine victory march past the spectators, a sergeant gave the order to halt, and the men commenced to set up camp not far from the village.

The officer-in-charge asked for the headman, who was among the crowd. 'Bring all people of English descent to meet me,' he said.

The headman put his hands together and bowed. 'Yes, sir.'

We ran home to give Mum the good news while the headman sent a messenger to relay the information to Dad.

After he left, Dad turned to Mum. 'Report to the officer, but don't ask him for anything. He'll expect a favour in return. You know what soldiers are like.'

Bertie escorted us to the camp and spoke to a sergeant, who pointed to an officer seated on a tree stump. A few soldiers stood guard. Further off, a group of Burmese craned their necks in an effort to catch the conversation.

Slim and handsome, the captain wore a moustache like Errol Flynn. When we approached, he stood and shook hands with Mum.

If only he would shake hands with me! But he didn't even glance my way. He asked whether we needed anything, but Mum said, 'I'm just so happy to see you.'

We need food, I wanted to scream. *We're starving.* I bit my tongue. I was terrified to go against Dad's wishes. Among the villagers who crowded around us were many of his relatives, who would report every word to him. Muslims were very strict with their womenfolk, and my father was a Muslim, though a non-practising one. And Mum, a Christian.

The Hand of God

After the interview, I remained behind with Bertie while Mum returned to the hut with Rose. We stood beneath the shade of a tamarind tree and watched the gunners mill around their twenty-pounders and feed shells into the guns' iron throats. The day was hot, and perspiration poured down their shirtless torsos as they worked. I admired their rippling muscles. We were all so skinny from starvation and had no muscles to speak of.

We shuddered as the guns spat out fire like great dragons.

The city of Mandalay had not yet been liberated as Japanese troops had taken refuge in the fort and dug deep bunkers in Mandalay Hill to make a stand there. Bertie told me the men were firing at Japanese troops, so I put my fingers to my ears and chuckled.

That evening, we returned to the hut, delirious with joy. Dad had somehow managed to obtain mepacrine tablets for Rupert's malaria, and he was sleeping soundly. By noon the following day, he rose from bed, looking like a ghost. His skin was yellow, and he appeared to have grown taller. Mum placed two buckets of water in the sun for him and, after a hot bath, he joined us for a meagre meal of fried rice. Rupert ate his food and licked his lips without taking his eyes off the plate. He didn't speak a word, but his appetite had returned, his indomitable spirit renewed. Mum's prayers had been answered.

Years later, I learned that America had wanted to reopen the Burma Road to transport military supplies into China. However, Churchill was intent on bypassing Burma, and regaining Malaya and Singapore. Fortunately for us, the US president managed to persuade him to concentrate on Burma first. Because of America's efforts to reconquer Northern Burma before the rest of Southeast Asia, Mandalay was liberated by the British in March 1945 after heavy street fighting.

If the Allies had postponed retaking Mandalay for a few months, Rupert would surely have died from malaria and his spirit would have been cut off in the spring of his life. Many of us also would have succumbed to starvation and sickness.

Despite the dangers of the Japanese occupation, the sickness and starvation we were subjected to, Rupert survived. The Lord had heard our prayers and placed his protecting hand over us.

My Dad

Ruth C Hall

My Dad: shearer and storyteller. He is no longer with us, but his legacy lives on in his five children, fourteen grandchildren and twenty-two great-grandchildren.

How often we as children would sit around our large family table after dinner, listening to his stories! He had a way about him; he'd take a tale and make us part of it. As kids we especially loved his shearing yarns, no matter if we had heard them over and over. So many incredible, true anecdotes which, eventually, my sister compiled into a book.

But there's one miraculous story that has had a lasting and, in fact, everlasting effect on my life and the lives of others of his descendants.

It was the late 1950s, and Dad knew little of God. Growing up in Adelaide, he'd had a dysfunctional childhood with many difficult issues, but found a certain peace working in the outback away from the crowds and busy cities. By his early 30s, he'd reached the pinnacle of his career as a sought-after and popular gun-shearer.

It was a tough life. Hard work, good money, and heavy drinking were fine for a few years. But it had evolved into an increasingly destructive pattern. He couldn't work without drinking; he couldn't play without the drink. He'd given up a few times, struggling with the horrendous effects of the DTs, but he always came back to needing the alcohol. He could still manage to work hard most weeks, but the weekends would be hour upon hour of covering up the increasing weight of wretchedness and despair by soaking in his inebriating painkiller.

One typical Sunday afternoon, when the pub had shut for the day, he continued drinking in his hotel room. Almost out of booze, his only option was to stagger down to the corner deli and buy some lemonade to stretch his supply a little longer. Desperate and alone, he would have been a pitiful sight.

With eyes downcast, he came to a small church where a service was finishing but found that, strangely, he just could not move past the entrance. It felt as if there was a solid glass wall and, however he tried, it was impossible to walk beyond that doorway. It seemed there was no option but to go inside. He stood at the back and listened to the pastor talk about Jesus and, when an altar call was given, my dad knew he wanted whatever they were offering. He walked down that aisle – a smelly, unwashed, unshaven shearer who'd been drinking for the past forty hours.

God met him that day. He was born again. Long story short, his alcoholism and smoking disappeared, he gave up his gambling, and God turned his life abruptly around. Within a year he found himself sitting next to a woman at church who eventually became his wife and my mother. One moment in a man's life determined the spiritual direction of his future generations.

My Dad: shearer, storyteller, beloved man of God.

An Unexpected Meeting

Francina Flemming

Remembrance Day 2021. We were in Newcastle, NSW, visiting our daughter, Angela, and her family. Our son Michael, who lives with us near the Queensland border, could not prepare his usual displays that mark this day in our household. Every Remembrance Day and Anzac Day he gathers from his storage cupboard his old and battered, authentic World War One bugle, his toy soldiers from childhood, and a World War One medal he found in an op shop.

The soldiers are lined up, his bugle and medal displayed, along with his grandfather's photo in military uniform taken during the Second World War. He arranges his presentation on the coffee table, or sometimes in our front yard hoping others might see it. Poppies, commemorative badges, rosemary from the garden, and any other memorabilia are proudly arranged.

Michael has a disability that limits his capacity to read but he knows his family stories well. He remembers the story of Uncle Stan, his great-grandmother's brother, who was a Lewis gunner, and died aged 21 at Villers-Bretonneux on 4th April 1918. He knows his grandfather was a soldier in the Second World War, and a Prisoner of War for four years. For Michael, to *remember* is a sacred duty on a sacred day.

We sensed his disappointment, the tension building in him because he could not prepare his display, so his sister Angela suggested we do the Anzac Walk at Bar Beach, Newcastle, hoping the walk would satisfy his expressed passion for this day to be remembered.

As we walked along the memorial pathway, Michael stopped at each memorial plaque. He could not read them but took lots of photos as I read them to him. After a while Angela and I walked ahead. His sister heard him loudly telling strangers walking by that it was 11o'clock and we needed to have a minute's silence. We walked back to him and stood in silence, then I recited the Ode and he joined with the response, 'We will remember them' and 'Lest we forget'.

I thought that would satisfy him, but he was not ready to move on. So we walked ahead again. I looked back and saw he was happily talking to a middle-aged couple. I retraced my steps and discovered Michael had searched his phone and found a recording of the Last Post which he was playing in solemn remembrance. The sound had attracted the couple's attention.

The woman, Meaghan, had been in the army for twenty years and explained how immediately she had heard the Last Post being played, she looked around, ready to snap to attention! Michael was so happy to get their interest and as she thanked him for remembering this day, so important to soldiers, we saw his tension dissipate. Meaghan explained that today was not only Remembrance Day, but also her birthday.

My husband Allan, Angela and I joined their conversation. I mentioned the book I had written about my father who was a Prisoner of War in WW2, and in answer to a question, I explained he was a signaller.

'No!' she exclaimed, 'I was in the signals too.' She wanted a book and I had some for sale in the motorhome nearby. But this was her birthday, and so a gift.

She and her partner walked with us to get the book and as I signed it she felt she needed to explain why she was wearing a mask, even when it wasn't mandated. 'I have a serious heart condition,' she shared.

I motioned to Angela, who said to her, 'I have three people in my family with heart conditions. Do you mind me asking what your problem is?'

Meaghan then explained her condition and that she had been told she probably needed a heart transplant. Angela and I smiled at each other. We knew this was another God-moment! My daughter then explained her family's story with three heart transplants: her husband, Lucas, transplanted just a year before, and two of her children, now eighteen and fifteen, who both needed heart transplants when they were thirteen. It turned out that Meaghan was under the same medical team in Sydney as Lucas, and Angela knew the medical team well.

What followed was, for Meaghan and her partner, a very helpful conversation and she expressed that 'we were meant to meet today'. She had been depressed and hadn't even wanted to get out of bed that morning. Her birthday morning! Meaghan had only come for this walk because her partner really encouraged her to do so. Now she had Angela's contact details if she wanted to talk more.

This had not been Angela's original plan for our day. It was going to be a bush walk far from here. We agreed that we also felt 'we were meant to be here today'. This Anzac Walk at Bar Beach was so different, a decision made because of Michael's strong feelings about Remembrance Day. His sister had changed her plans to help him cope with his disappointment.

That morning, as Angela had finished her morning coffee she had prayed, 'God, what do you want me to do today?' And God directed her to this walk.

I love every experience God sends that displays his gracious love and mercy. As Shakespeare says, it drops like gentle rain on those who experience it. Refreshing, renewing, and life-giving. God's mercy was in evidence again today as we walked with him; to Michael, to Meaghan and to each of us who were part of this story.

Outside the Fold

June Hopkins

An urgent knock at the door, late on a cold rainy night, had me immediately thinking of an emergency. I opened the door a fraction, then wider as I saw the face of our pastor. Immediately in front of him was a barefoot, bedraggled, teenage girl.

'Police found this young woman in the local park, trying to sleep in a picnic shelter. Driving past the church they saw the lights were still on, so they brought her in to see if I knew someone who might give her a bed for the night.' He spoke quickly, grimacing oddly at me behind her back. 'She doesn't seem to have any possessions,' he added.

I looked more critically at the teenager, noting that she was scowling. She flashed angry eyes in my direction, reminding me of a trapped animal. Her stance was hostile and defensive, and had it not been raining so heavily, I think she would have run away from us, right there and then.

'You have teenage girls,' the pastor continued, 'so I thought you might be willing to have her stay here.'

'Of course she can stay. What's your name, lass?' I asked, trying to sound more accepting than I felt. My teenagers were naïve, well-loved innocents. In those few seconds the girl stood before me, thoughts of drug addiction and rebelliousness coloured in the larger picture, accurately or not. I was always nervous about my own offspring coming in close contact with or being influenced by someone like her.

The pastor shook his head. 'She refuses to tell us her name.' The girl did not answer my question.

I thanked the pastor and led her into the house.

'Are you hungry?' She nodded, so I began making her some toast. After she had eaten, I suggested a warm shower might make her feel better, feeling thankful when she said 'Okay.' I found her some pyjamas and showed her the bathroom.

By now, my own seventeen-year-old daughter had arisen and come to see what the noise was all about. She generously offered to give up her room for the night, saying she would sleep on the sofa.

When the girl emerged, a difference in her demeanour was evident. She hung her head when I introduced her to my daughter, but I saw her shoulders had relaxed and I glimpsed the hint of a smile. Perhaps she realised she was safe.

'You can call me Sandy,' she said, 'but that's not my real name.' I sighed with relief at the change in her attitude, and that she had spoken without prompting.

After she was safely bedded down, I climbed into my own bed and thought about the situation.

'Where are you, Lord, in all of this? What do you want of me?'

His answer was fast. 'Remember the ninety-nine sheep that were safe, but one was out in the cold and lost? That lamb is this child.' I got the message. The Bible uses the term 'fold' to describe the place where sheep are together, sheltered, and safe. The lost lamb, in the biblical story, was nowhere near the fold. My family and I needed to be the hands and feet of Jesus to this girl, enfolding her with his love. It sounded so simple, but the arrival of the next day showed me that we were traversing rough terrain with this lost lamb.

Rather than eat breakfast, Sandy asked me for money so that she could go buy some cigarettes. I was challenged about what it means to love unconditionally. Was it the Holy Spirit that prompted me to give her the money? I gave her twenty dollars, having no idea of the cost of cigarettes. She asked directions to the local shops. As she went, I was certain she wouldn't return, but she did.

For the rest of the day, she sat under the gazebo in our back yard, puffing her way through the packet. I tried hard to engage her further in conversation, but she gave nothing away. I had no inkling as to where she lived, why she was homeless, or if she was in trouble. She limited her conversation to sharing about the difficulties of living rough, her speech littered with swearing and expletives. Alone with her, my daughter had a little more success with gleaning information. Sandy revealed to her she had an abusive stepfather whom she refused to live with. She had much younger siblings who took up most of her mother's time.

Reading between the lines in the limited conversations she had, my daughter deduced there had been a big fight in the home, following which Sandy had run away. For the past several weeks she had been living on the streets.

I prayed much more than usual because I didn't know what to do. The truth was that I did not want her to stay with my family for long because her rough language, street-smart attitude and addictive behaviour might negatively impact my daughters. I wrestled with God about letting her stay. My mind repeatedly returned to the lost sheep. Eventually I achieved a peace about the situation when I heard God say, 'Trust me.'

Sandy seemed to be settling in, when on the third day she suddenly revealed that her mother had a part-time job working in a shop a few suburbs away. I offered to drive her there to see her mother, which is what I thought she was angling for. Perhaps a taste of family life again had softened her attitude.

She agreed so long as I went into the shop with her. In clothes and shoes loaned by my daughter, and with her hair neatly combed, Sandy appeared both excited and apprehensive to be seeing her mother.

After attracting her mother's attention, we waited until there were no customers. Initially, Sandy's mother was distinctly cold towards her. She also looked me up and down with a dismissive stare. When Sandy began to cry, her mother's stoic composure broke, and she reached out to her for a hug.

'I am not coming home,' Sandy said. 'I can't live with him, but I'll stay in touch, Mum.' That was the end of the interaction.

Driving back to my place, I offered to help her find somewhere suitable to stay. I shared with her that she mattered to God, and he was there for her, with answers for her if she turned to him. She gave me a sceptical smile in response.

Over the next few days, I sought accommodation options for her, but Sandy was reluctant and too restless to commit to any resolution. Then, exactly a week after she had arrived, I woke one morning to find her bed was empty. She had left us overnight. A note on her pillow thanked us for helping her and for the 'God stuff'.

I realised then that we had been asked to plant a seed. In my quiet time I reflected on 1 Corinthians 3 verse 6. One plants the seed, another waters it but it is God who makes it grow. I continued to pray for her, asking God to send others along to water that seed, with the hope that eventually there would be the growth of faith in him.

Outside the Fold

A couple of years later, she recognised me at a shopping centre and rushed over to greet me. She was pushing a pram and was already a young mother. She seemed happy, emotionally together, and capable. There was no apology for her sudden departure, but she assured me she had been helped by other 'God people' after she left. Sandy did not claim to have become a Christian, but I saw that her journey with God was still an active work in progress.

This happened years ago, and I never encountered her again. However, a recent event reminded me of the inner conflict I experienced over Sandy. I was approached in the supermarket by a healthy-looking, scruffy teenage boy. He asked me for money. It was another one of those times when I was confronted with the question of how willing I was to be used by God, when what was being asked of me brought disquiet to my psyche. Determining my responsibilities to those 'outside the fold', especially when they are on a path contrary to that which seems healthy and honourable to me, remains a challenge.

Blue

Roslyn Bradshaw

The cosmetics case is blue, the colour of sky, of the sea, of the blue bird of happiness. Those crazy seventies memes: *May the bluebird of happiness nest in your hair.*

My older sister Chris and I were home in Wudinna for the Christmas holidays, after a year in Port Lincoln, she teaching junior primary children and me studying Year 11 at high school. My two sisters and I were very blue, mourning, drearily packing, separating treasures, choosing which loss could be borne. We were moving but we didn't know exactly where to. Dad was a manager for the State Bank and our fate was being decided in Adelaide by bank executives. We felt like pawns in a giant game of 'move the manager'. Frantic tidying proceeded as the new school year loomed. I had English assignments to complete and post back to Port Lincoln, as tension built about our deployment. Was it worth even doing a Dickens paper which Mr. Olesnikiy was so finicky about? After another blue at the dinner table, I burst into tears.

My older sister Chris pointed accusingly at Dad, 'See! Now look what you've done!'

Our indignation rose up. Chris felt the anguish, heaping up from Karoonda to Meningie, Meningie to Maitland, Maitland to Wudinna, now Wudinna to who knew where. Each move was another parting.

'We're not happy. We don't want to leave things behind. When I'm a parent, I'm not making my kids throw out their treasures.'

Blue

She might have been throwing her words at a brick wall and Mum just shook her head sadly, not meeting our eyes. Dad was firm, stoic. 'You know the bank won't pay for us to move all this stuff.' He never gave us an inch, no matter how much Chris shouted and argued. I was a silent witness, an ineffectual deputy.

'One cardboard box each.'

Three years of collecting, fossicking, making, creating, loving, and playing cannot be jammed into one small cardboard box. We grieved as we sorted. We muttered and moaned in the dark after lights out. Little sister Lyn recalled her previous act of rebellion, sequestering a blackboy hobby horse in a wardrobe so her friend could move to Wudinna with her.

Chris tried again, 'We need more boxes. It's not fair to make us throw all our stuff out. What about my college notes, my…?'

Chris was a country schoolteacher now. Teacher's College had given her some spunk. Taught her to believe in herself and her agency. She had fluffed out from a timid fledgling in the nest to a full-grown adult, albeit without a nest. She boarded with kindly country folk in return for teaching their chicks. Her belongings now included important things like books, flashcards and cards scrawled with, 'I love you, Miss Longmire.' Chris needed the 'Dump of Mum and Dad' more than the 'Bank of Mum and Dad' at this point in her life. She had no fixed address.

Suddenly there was a reprieve. We weren't shifting now. *Really? Wow!*

We relaxed, relieved. Chris left on the bus and Lyn and I were still under orders to reduce, tidy, and pack. My English paper came back in the post covered with corrections and new instructions. It looked like I'd be doing Matriculation at my beloved Port Lincoln High School after all.

Blue. Blues. Blues rhythm. Are jazz and blues twins? Blue sky. Bluebird. In dreams blue symbolises spirituality. In the Bible blue is the colour of heaven. In Wudinna they call me Blue because I'm a redhead.

Blue. I have the cosmetics case still. I don't use it, but to me it represents acceptance and friendship. I remember the story so well, my year on an emotional rollercoaster. Thoughts flick back and forth. Memories. An insecure girl from Wudinna, being embraced into a melting pot of girls in the Bush Church Aid Hostel, and into a high school whose 1,000 pupils doubled the population of my entire tiny country town. There had been twelve in my Year 10 class at Wudinna, with only one other girl. I had to go to Port Lincoln if I wanted to continue my education, but it had been a frightening prospect. I could win the Senior Girls Cup and break all the athletics records in Wudinna. Could I win a single race in Port Lincoln? Could I be a big fish in a big pond? Or a medium-sized fish in a big pond?

In Port Lincoln, I put my head down and studied hard, worked hard, trained hard. I was uncertain of acceptance, but small signs were encouraging. I was elected as a prefect after only one year. Winning the Senior Girls Cup opened the door to lead Eyre House despite my inability to march in a straight line. Mrs Needle, the PE teacher, told me I needed a compass to swim the length of the pool. Country girls didn't need straight lines. They needed bush lore. But then the Matric rabble lads categorised me in the 'cool' group. I had made it. I had come home. I was not an outsider from up the bush. I finally belonged.

I had applied to be a Rotary exchange student, to spend a year in Japan staying with host families. I had the first interview coming up. They wanted to meet me, and Dad had to meet them too.

Then out of the blue it came. A bombshell.

'We're moving to Loxton, and you're coming with us. In two weeks. I'm coming down tomorrow to get you. We will leave after the interview with the Rotarians,' Dad says flatly on the telephone.

Suddenly my paper castles crumpled around me and I would be packing again. Everything I'd built in the past fourteen months swept away. I was numb with shock. I put down the phone and went to our bedroom. This time my emotions, newly massaged and pampered, took over. I cried. I wailed. I cried again.

'You're moving? Now? What about the exams? Your music exams?'

'Our shindig plans?'

Everyone was sympathetic. Even the hostel parents were supportive. We were drowning in blues. All I could think of was what I must leave behind, of what I had to lose. For the first time in my life, I knew despair. I knew blue not as the colour of heaven but of despair.

In the morning I got up, had breakfast and got ready for netball in a daze. Once on the court, I forgot everything and we won convincingly. I got 'best and fairest' on the court but I could not bask in the glory. I would never play with them again. My life was over. So sad. So blue.

Mum and Dad came for lunch. I couldn't look at them. I was a prisoner being taken away.

Dad went into Graham's office, where punishment was meted out to recalcitrant girls. Maybe he could be my advocate with my father.

God, help me! My prayer winged its way to heaven.

Chris rang me. She was fighting mad. She had suffered so much from being uprooted when she was in the middle of Year 10. She didn't want this to happen to me. She was a comforting ally, but an impotent one, I felt. I went numbly to the Rotary meeting.

Diary entry: Saturday 2 April.
> *The interview that evening with the Rotary President went okay. It was not formidable. On the way back to the hostel Dad said I could stay if I wanted to. I jumped up and down with joy. Everyone else is pleased. Heather, Liz, and I stayed up talking past lights out.*

I never found out why Dad changed his mind. Was it Graham, or Chris, or kind Mr Beer from the Rotary Club? I just know God heard my cry. We never spoke of it again, an embarrassing blue buried with my father. Later we had a much better relationship, but some things seemed better forgotten.

The day after Dad changed his mind, a surprise party. The unexpected parcel was a weird shape. I looked around at the hostel parents, the thirty girls, and then at my three roommates, stunned. I was perplexed to be receiving a gift.

'Go on, open it,' a junior kid yelled.

A happy day, when I didn't have to leave my life here. A blue-sky day when a stylish blue cosmetics case with a silver inscribed plate eased its way into my group of never-to-be-discarded possessions. They must have arranged it when everyone thought I was leaving. I was embarrassed. My eyes filled with tears.

Blue is the colour of acceptance and friendship.

> To Roslyn
>
> With Best Wishes
>
> From the Girls
>
> B C A Hostel Port Lincoln
>
> 1969-70

The Test
Teri Kempe

My friend was sick. Her faith was wavering. I prayed for her, both for healing and renewal of her faith. I am blessed with good health, hardly a day of sickness all my life. I asked God if I ever became sick, would he help me always to trust him? I could not have imagined the adventure I was about to experience.

I fly from Sydney to Brisbane for a long-awaited (Covid-interrupted) holiday with my dear friend Elly. The joy of our reunion is sweet. Three days later an invitation to a church retreat is gratefully accepted. As the leader encourages us to release our worries and relax, I feel the room begin to swim. Is it a claustrophobia attack? What is happening to me?

I stagger out of the room – sweating, shivering and nauseous. Quickly aided by an attendee who is also a nurse; she calls an ambulance. The local hospital cannot accept an emergency and I am sped across town to Princess Alexandra Hospital. My first experience in an ambulance. I had not been in hospital since giving birth to my last child forty years before.

Drifting in and out of consciousness, I hardly remember the admission. I surface to find myself in a four-bed ward with three elderly gentlemen. Endless tests – is this also my spiritual test, I wonder? Diagnosis: pancreatitis and gall stones. I'd heard this was very painful but I feel little pain. No doubt drugs are helping.

Endone makes me hallucinate. I am talking to people not there, yet their image is so clear. The compassionate care of the nursing staff is magnificent. Doctors come every day and detail my progress and what to expect. Everything is meticulously recorded on my computer record. The wonders of modern technology. Each doctor or nurse could read my history.

PAH is a teaching hospital and three students interview me. What a privilege to watch these young doctors in training develop their bedside manner and explore the personal journey of the patients to which they are assigned. They do well.

Two sons travel from Sydney bringing love and warmth of the family. The doctors vacillate – should they operate in Brisbane or send me to Sydney? They try to flush out the gallstones, filling me with fluid that goes to the wrong places – my lungs – while my heart races. I cannot be moved – the stones will not be flushed.

Let's wait and see. The journey would be dangerous, with no guarantee there would not be another attack. I'm so grateful for the professionalism of the surgeons. At last they make the decision to operate in Brisbane in the hospital which has all my records and knows my history. It's a waiting game.

Elly visits with flowers, takes my washing. This is not what we planned for our holiday. Thank you, Elly. You are a true friend.

Ten days after admission my fluid levels are down – ten kilos of fluid discarded, and finally my oxygen levels are safe to operate. I am prepped. Nil by mouth. Early morning surgery. But then I hear the helicopter landing on the helipad nearby. A happy recipient of a suitable liver draws all staff and theatres. An eight hour transplant operation causes all else to be cancelled. Still they say it might happen for me today. I doubt it. I am hungry but feel completely at peace. I am in God's hands.

'Time to go.' It is 3pm. A wardsman appears and gives me five minutes to get ready. Wheeled in my own bed, I am in a trance. Down the corridor and into the lift to the operating theatre on the floor below. Endless questions. Name, date of birth. Is this in case I forget who I am?

'Do you have anything in your body you weren't born with?'

'Yes – the Holy Spirit'.

'Do you have dentures, crowns?'

'No, I'm waiting for heaven for my crown.'

The surgeon smiles and the nurse squeezes my hand. She knows.

I pray for the surgeon, anaesthetist and nurse as they explain the details of what is going to happen. I peer through the glass doors. It's like a spaceship. Huge multi-faceted lights. Bright white walls.

I feel no qualms, no butterflies, just an eager anticipation and confirmation that Jesus is with me. He is tangibly present.

Wheeled closer to the operating theatre door, I notice the name – Operating Theatre C3.

'That's the name of my church – now I know Jesus is with me.'

There can be only one reason for this surreal calm I feel – the Holy Spirit envelops me. I seem to be riding on a cloud of prayers.

'How are you feeling?'

'Excited!'

'Oh, that's an unusual answer.'

They wheel me in and I wriggle onto the narrow operating table. Still no qualms. A surreal sense of being held by Jesus.

As the mask is placed over my mouth: 'Count down from ten'.

'Ten, nine...' Oblivion.

The Test

I wake up to a nurse telling me all is well, no complications. Gall bladder and stones removed by key hole surgery.

'Praise the Lord! Thank you, Jesus.'

Twenty-four hours later I am discharged. Covid staff shortages necessitate this. My youngest son reappears to take me home. He brings love and support from home: five children, their spouses and fifteen grandchildren. My church is praying, my friends are earnestly seeking my healing. I know it. I am loved.

Oh no. It's the State of Origin football game– not a bed to be found in Brisbane.

I wait in a wheelchair in the hospital lobby. After hundreds of calls to Airbnb, motels and hotels, at last a bed is found, for one night only. I cannot fly for four days. We arrive at an inner-city hotel for a restful night.

Next morning check out is 10am and check in to the next place not until 2pm. Sitting on a park bench, I long to lie down. Thankfully my son thinks of the State Library. At least there is a comfy chair where I can just sit. Concentration is hard. My mind wanders. Oh, for a bed! Finding a little nook in the café, I take a nap. I'm conscious that my son, who runs a very busy start-up company, is sacrificing so much to be with me. Thank you, family. His four little ones, seven, five, three and one, are missing him terribly, not to mention his wife.

After four days, at last we check into the airport. A welcome wheelchair at 10am but flight not until 5pm. I find a vacant waiting area and take a nap. So good!

First on the plane, last off. Thank you, Qantas. So good to be home. But the cost of these four days is almost three thousand dollars...no cheap flights, and extraordinary accommodation costs. I have a grateful heart for all who contributed to cover costs.

Did I pass the test? I think so...I can trust him to take care of me. He is faithful – I am safe. Thank you, Jesus! Next time, Elly, we'll have a real holiday.

Sparks of Grace
Tony Koch

As a post-war migrant from the former Yugoslavia, I grew up facing many challenges, but I have always had a sense of God's watchful presence over me. But it was through my trade as an electrician that God showed me his grace most powerfully.

From the refugee settlement community in Cowra, NSW, I received an apprenticeship as an electrician in Sydney. My first job was at the Children's Hospital in Camperdown. What an experience that was, working with a range of tradies including plumbers, brickies, carpenters, painters and fellow electricians among others. The language used and jokes told were a shock to my system. I wondered why God had led me there.

When work on the hospital was completed, an open day was organised for the mayor and other local 'big wigs'. In preparation for this, the foreman, Bill, asked me to go to the main switchboard room in the basement and clean and dust all the switchboard gear and wiring I had earlier helped to install, as this room was to be on the inspection tour. The main power for the hospital came through the electrical switchboard from a nearby power sub-station with three-phase high voltage cables. The wires I was cleaning would be very hot indeed when turned on!

As I was going about the cleaning, the boss, Mr Halloway, came into the room, took one look at me, and turned white as a ghost. He had just been at the power sub-station, had his hand on the main power switch, and was about to turn on the power to the hospital. But something didn't feel right and he hesitated, then decided to go to the hospital and check that the door to the switchboard room was closed and locked – just to be on the safe side. Imagine his shock and surprise to find me there with my hands on the wires. If he had thrown the switch, I would have been killed instantly. I experienced God's grace that day in a very concrete way. But God was not yet done teaching me about his grace.

Even though our home had a Christian background, I knew little about the Bible. English was my second language and I found the old King James Bible by mother had acquired incomprehensible. Again, it was through my work as an electrician that God showed me his grace.

After completing my apprenticeship, I found myself back in Cowra, where one of my first jobs was at the local Christian bookshop. The lady in charge, for some reason, felt compelled to give me a Good News version of the Bible. Once I started to read it, I could not put it down. When I came across a word I did not understand, I asked a friend. Through reading that Bible I learned about the gracious God who had earlier spared my life. It was the beginning of a life-long journey with the God of grace.

Meeting the Light
Glenda Austin

It was the chocolate biscuits and the dark green GI lime cordial that we found exciting. We didn't get those sugary treats at home. We had home-made Anzac biscuits and, when we were a bit older, Mum made a chocolate slice I loved.

There were monkey bars in the back yard too. At home, we only had bits and pieces we could build cubbies with, usually under the peach tree. I would climb a bigger tree in the corner of the yard sometimes.

I don't remember how we got to the house for this After School Club. It was an ordinary kind of house not far away from ours. Mum must have driven us there and I only remember going that once. After all, 1963 was a long time ago. After the biscuits and cordial and playing in the yard, we all sat in the living room on the floor. I was eleven, my sister nine.

Why I responded is still a mystery to me. I don't think I had ever seen anything supernatural at that point. Sure, I knew the difference between fantasy and reality. I know now that children usually grasp that by about age five. I well knew the difference. I didn't believe in fairies, and in the games I played I actually wanted things to be a real as possible. I built real floors in cubbies and my doll had a real fur stole – fur I ripped off a toy monkey. I liked to set the stage for play but didn't enjoy the game so much – I didn't like to 'pretend'. There was less in the way of fantasy on television then. Of course, there were some fictional shows and characters to watch: 'Superman', 'Mr Ed' the talking horse, and cartoons. I read imaginative stories. Yet supernatural things were never real to me. Until that day when I met the Light.

The supernatural is very real to me now. Not seen everywhere and not all the time, but there. I have known healings come to pass, I have seen accidents avoided or no harm come to those involved. Known lives saved. Issues resolved. Small successes. I have been told of things to come and in time they have proved true. I have had gifts of knowledge and wisdom and I have had financial blessings and answers to prayers many times in many ways.

On that day when I met the Light, I don't know why I believed what I saw to be supernatural. It doesn't hold up now when I tell others. It could be easily explained as a natural phenomenon although, to me, after years of knowing the Light, I am sure it was truly not a natural or coincidental thing.

Called in for a story, we sat there, a giant grey felt board propped up so we could all see it. There were many cut out things on the board. The woman began to tell us about Jesus. She was speaking about examples from the Bible and pointing to the pictures that illustrated the verses. There was a picture of a lantern like an old kerosene lamp. She began to quote from John 8: 'I am the light of the world. He who follows me shall not walk in darkness but have the light of life'. As she spoke and pointed, a stray sunbeam somehow shot through the closed blind and curtains and hit just that picture. It glowed. The woman saw this, and tears filled her eyes. I saw. Saw this was a supernatural emphasis God had created and I read the message too.

A little later when she asked us to close our eyes and then to put a hand up if we wanted to ask Jesus into our heart. I raised my hand and peeked enough to see my sister had too.

That was how I met the Light of the world. He came into my heart at that point. He has drawn me close many times. I have walked away from him many times, sometimes for years. Still he loves me.

It occurred to me only recently that I certainly have had a strange connection to things 'After School', like that club. I may not be serving GI cordial or stories about Jesus, but I have worked in After School Care for around thirty years now. I think the cliché, 'Bloom where you are planted' could apply.

Throughout the long years of my life, I have seen miracles and the Light of God moving in ways that are much more complex and unexplainable than that first sunbeam experience. The comfort and the joy God has given me has balanced the sad and the tragic of life and I am ever grateful for meeting the Light that day, and growing in the relationship that is both supernatural and real.

Bones and Blue Eyes
RJ Rodda

I often get compliments for my blue eyes despite their irregular hazel streaks. During high school, I accepted those compliments with a polite smile and an inner bitterness because those much-praised eyes did not see very well.

When I failed my first eye test in Year 8, my initial response was anger. I told the health professional I had failed because I'd left the bright outdoor sun to enter the gloomy portable building where the tests were held. 'My eyes just need longer to adjust to the light,' I insisted.

By the following year, I had admitted to myself that my eyesight was deteriorating. I could only see the board at school if I sat in the front row, but I didn't want to sit in the front row. I wanted to sit with my friends and I didn't want to tell them, or anybody else, that I was having trouble seeing. I didn't want my friends to become front-row 'skoogs' for me or worse, ditch me so that I sat alone.

Instead, I developed a variety of strategies so that my poor eyesight would go undetected. If there was work to copy down from the board, I would squint at it first, to try and make the letters clearer. If that didn't work, I would sneak peeks at my friends' work or those nearby. If worst came to worst, I would take something to the bin by the teacher's desk, to get a closer look at the words I could not read.

Then one day I was publicly exposed, in maths class of all places. My maths teacher was Mrs D, a short dynamic woman who regretted not choosing a more brilliant career. 'Aim to be the boss, not to work for a boss,' she preached.

One day Mrs D pointed to a maths equation on the board and asked me what the answer was. I was sitting three rows back from the front and couldn't see it. I squinted before saying, 'I don't know.'

'Can you read the question?' she snapped back. I flushed, humiliated in front of all my classmates.

That night I admitted my need to my mother, who also has short-sighted blue eyes. I was taken to the optometrist and fitted for a pair of most unattractive glasses. I have a square face and the glasses were too round and too small to look good on me. I tried to wear contact lenses and, after a number of tries, mastered putting them in, but they made the rims of my eyelids turn red and often felt uncomfortable.

As a teenager returning to the Christian faith of my childhood, I prayed and prayed and prayed that God would heal my eyes.

One day on a family holiday we visited a random church. There the visiting speaker asked if anyone wanted prayer for healing. I put my hand up and asked him to pray for my eyes. He did so but then with microphone in hand, he asked if I could see any better. Under the scrutiny of many strangers, I scrunched my eyes to try to see clearer.

'A bit,' I said into the microphone. Everyone was pleased but after I left the church it became apparent to me that my eyesight had not improved. In fact, each time I went to the optometrist my prescription grew stronger.

Years later, I was invited to go with some friends to Ballarat for a special healing meeting. Pastor Roy was to be the speaker.

We drove three hours to get there and sat at the back of a crowded traditional-style church building. When Pastor Roy asked if anyone wanted prayer, I stood up as did many other people. I waited as Pastor Roy prayed for person after person ahead of me. Finally, it was my turn. My turn to be prayed for. My turn to be healed.

He laid his hands on me and I felt a warm and joyful presence envelop me. Then to my surprise, Pastor Roy told me to put my hands on my hip bones. I did so. He placed his hands on the top of mine before praying that God would move my hips back into position. Beneath my fingers something shifted. Then Pastor Roy went on to pray for someone else.

I'd never thought anything was wrong with my hip bones. They stuck out like chicken wings, but I thought that was normal. Yet often I would run my hands up and down the sides of my body, feeling how my hip bones were a jarring bump on an otherwise flat run.

This random prayer astonished me, but I was on the ground now, with no recollection of falling, a tremendous happiness flooding through me, curving my lips upwards until they could stretch no further.

Eventually it was time to get up. As I rose unsteadily, I noted that my eyes were the same as always, but I was very curious about my hip bones. Had God really moved them? Why would he do that? I went to the bathroom and checked, running my hands along my body as I always did. To my amazement, my hip bones were now neatly tucked in. Stunned, I left the bathroom.

Later on, I told my story to a paramedic, who said that if your hip bones stick out you can have trouble having babies and may need corrective surgery. I still don't know if that is true or not, but during my many years of being single, I held on to that like a promise: that God must want me to have babies, else why would he fix my body?

And my eyes? Years later, I heard of corrective laser surgery. The surgery was a new thing and I held off, afraid of what would happen if something went wrong. I would wake up seeing only my husband, the rest of the room a blur before I groped around and found my glasses.

After yet another depressing eye check-up where I was told my prescription had once again worsened, I looked into laser surgery. I became convinced it was safe, and my husband was supportive.

My eyes hurt after the operation but a day later I had twenty-twenty vision. The world was clear and sharp and bright and I gloried in it.

I now have excellent vision, flat hip bones and three children. And if I ever doubt God is real or good, I can run my hands down the sides of my body and feel a miracle.

Emerging from the Fog
Craig Chapman

Futility was gathering momentum as daylight fought valiantly to overcome the darkness of a crisp autumn morning. It was obvious that we would not be glimpsing the sun for some time. In fact, anything not directly illuminated by our car's headlights was going to remain hidden for quite a while. The sea of fog in which we were immersed seemed ruthlessly determined to strangle the encroaching light before it could take effect.

The location of our accommodation had prompted Google maps to direct us via the back roads rather than straight to the main highway. Our frightfully early start, in anticipation of the long day ahead, meant that we were now experiencing this suffocating fog in its full measure. The valleys and depressions north of Canberra provided a vast array of basins in which the dense, seemingly impenetrable substance could take up residence. The eeriness was highlighted at each bend in the road, as fences, gates, trees and sheep emerged ghost-like from the shrouded landscape.

A feeling of deja vu now gripped me. Not that my physical location or surroundings were well known to me; it was the sense of groping around in an unseen world, searching frantically for a way forward which was so familiar. I had recently experienced two years of metaphorical fog. Throughout that time, I had no idea of when it would lift.

Many people automatically associate a boarding school education with privilege. Comparatively few are aware of the hidden story of trauma which often accompanies it. Even many survivors themselves remain unable to acknowledge the damage which has been inflicted on them. Until three years ago, I was such a person.

My traumatic boarding school experience officially began when I was twelve, although the plan that I was destined to continue this family tradition was confirmed from my infancy. Far from preparing me for what lay ahead, this only served to initiate the process of isolating me from my peers and home community well before the actual physical separation. The fact that I went from one of the state's smallest rural primary schools to one of its largest, most imposing and affluent private schools certainly didn't help.

Technically, it ended just before my seventeenth birthday. At least, that was when the crushing sense of abandonment and the trauma associated with living in a hostile environment without the love and security of family and home ended. The bullying and intimidation of my school years were over at that point. But it didn't really end there at all. The isolation, disconnection, denial and inability to process what had happened continued for almost forty years.

There were numerous casualties. One of the earliest was the loss of the family farm. Like many firstborn farming sons, I harboured an ambition to follow the path forged by previous generations – five, in my case. This dream was soon shattered. It wasn't that I didn't have the opportunity to inherit the farm. I was simply too disconnected from my home community to make it a reality. So, still only seventeen, I left the district, pretending that I didn't want to be a farmer, and focussed on the need to hide my trauma. Perhaps only those raised on the land can fully comprehend the implications of making such a momentous decision at such a young age.

Only recently have I begun to come to terms with the ongoing trauma which my denial imposed on me. From an external point of view, I suppose my coverup was somewhat successful. I managed to keep my past hidden from the majority of people I interacted with. However, I paid an enormous price and the damage which was inflicted mounted over the years. Throughout those four decades I never spoke willingly of my experience and *absolutely* never revealed any details. I carefully plotted every aspect of my life to make sure my trauma remained hidden. Many people who thought they knew me quite well knew nothing about the trauma. Perhaps only my amazingly patient and longsuffering wife knew it existed and even she only knew what her powers of observation revealed, due to my steadfast refusal to talk.

My forty years in the wilderness ended with what some might call a change of heart. I prefer to think of it as a miraculous intervention in which God gently revealed my brokenness and led me to a place where it was safe for me to open up and seek help. The initial breakthrough came in the form of a simple but profound revelation from my counsellor. 'It wasn't your fault' was his conclusion to my hour-and-a half-long, clumsy initial attempt to verbalise what had happened to me. It changed everything. I had never contemplated such a reality and had, in fact, spent those forty years blaming myself. I knew immediately I was on a pathway to recovery.

Ironically, however, the beginning of my recovery also marked the onset of the fog. Although I was finally experiencing freedom from the burden I had carried, the process of redefining my life in relation to a previously undisclosed trauma was quite overwhelming. For the next two years I struggled to find a way forward, to get a clear view of my past and form a coherent story about the whole ordeal. Although I now *wanted* to tell my story, I found it difficult that many of those I confided in struggled to relate to an experience which was so foreign to theirs. I began to despair as the fog of isolation closed in. Then, after a time, God spoke again in a quiet, almost imperceptible voice…

Fogs don't last forever. They always lift. This, too, will lift.

As we approached the Hume Highway to continue our long journey home, cresting the various undulations of the terrain, sunlight began to penetrate and the density of the fog decreased. The way ahead became clearer as visibility improved. Soon we were driving through bright, early morning sunshine, confident of much more favourable conditions ahead. Though the fog had resisted stubbornly for a time, the sun was able to break through as it always does. Despite the much longer time period, the pattern during my two years of coming to terms with previously unacknowledged trauma was similar.

There were a couple of key breakthroughs during the trauma fog's final months. My wife and I attended a family reunion, enabling us to spend a weekend exploring the rural community in which I had spent my youth. It had been many years since I'd spent significant time in the location, thinking about what had happened. The grief associated with being forced to leave the family farm at a young age had been buried for decades as I had tried desperately to hide my trauma. Now, at the first signs of the fog lifting, I was finally able to grieve that loss. The reunion itself included a stark reminder of my farming heritage. For the first time, rather than guilt, I felt the release of knowing that my inability to follow the footsteps of my predecessors was not my fault.

As I continued the long-suppressed process of grieving the loss of the farm, God nudged me to act on something else that needed attention. I had benefited from an extended period of counselling in the early stages of my recovery. Feeling that it had run its course, I had not presented for counselling for quite a while. It was time for some more. This time around, I had a particular focus in relation to the process. The isolation resulting from the understandable inability of most people to identify with my traumatic experience had enabled the fog to continue its suffocating tendencies. It was this I needed help with. Over the course of several counselling sessions, I began to understand two different categories of pain which I had borne. Like everyone, I carried "clean" pain, the unavoidable impact of my unique circumstances. But I had held on to far too much "dirty" pain; the extra burden that I had unnecessarily clung to.

Eventually, I came to terms with the idea that I could accept the reality of the clean pain and let go of the dirty stuff which was inhibiting my recovery. Finally, the fog was lifting.

The journey toward healing continues. It is a long, slow process. I expect it to be a life-long one. For now, the way ahead is much clearer, as is the view behind me. I have emerged from the fog. Perhaps there will be other fogs to contend with in the future.

Even if there are, I know the sun will break through eventually. I thank God that fogs don't last forever.

Love and Lemon Cake

Steph Penny

My friend recently made me a lemon cake. And I cried.

Usually, the sight of cake does not make me cry (although a delicious slice of cake can certainly move me). But love and acts of kindness from good friends will bring on the tears – especially when such gestures are given unexpectedly.

On this occasion, my friend had made a memorial cake for my recently-departed furbaby. Portia had died at the age of nineteen, having lived with me for seventeen years. My cat had been more than a pet: she was a confidante, comforter, playmate and companion. She helped me survive many painful years of loneliness and sickness, and I often felt God bringing me his peace through her.

She was a literal Godsend.

My friend knew that. She knew how much my furbaby meant to me. She was so saddened to hear of the passing of my beloved Portia that she baked me a lemon cake.

Why a lemon cake? Because Portia is now buried in the backyard under a lemon tree.

I looked at the cake positioned in the centre of the table, little curls of lemon rind perched on the top, and felt the tears well up. 'Thank you,' I choked.

But there was more; my friend wasn't finished yet. She giggled mischievously and handed me a bag full of lemon-themed gifts and goodies, including a folder of lemon-related recipes with contributions from several people at church. When I learned that a group of people had been moved to help memorialise Portia, the tears trickled down my cheeks.

What a sweet way to remember my sweet girl.

We ate cake in weepy contentment that afternoon. (It was a delicious cake too.) It occurred to me that grief is a peculiar beast. It is sometimes subtle, sometimes overwhelming, but I find it is always better when shared. That day, I felt like my friends had come alongside me to share my grief. I felt like they cared, like they really loved me. And I felt like I was truly part of God's family in a tangible and unmistakable way.

You will be glad to know the lemon tree is currently thriving in its position above Portia, and has already produced fresh lemons. I have both lemons and lemon recipes to keep her memory alive.

The Battle for Libby
Ruth C Hall

The Three Sisters lookout at the iconic Blue Mountains in New South Wales is forever etched in my mind as a place where God stepped in to protect a precious gift he had given me. My sister and I were on a road trip with my four-month-old baby Libby in tow. We'd broken our long journey with a little sight-seeing on the way, this being one of our stops.

Walking along the pathway amongst the soaring eucalypt trees and lush forest, the sounds of a variety of birds surrounded us. It was so peaceful, giving me no inkling of the horrifying incident that was soon to unravel. As we approached the viewing platform, we passed a group of sightseers leaving, making us the only ones in this lofty, almost celestial space. The vista was spectacular, taking in the huge mountain range which included the three enormous rock formations that rose nearly one kilometre above sea level. The panorama took our breath away as we gazed in awe across the stunning, picturesque valley.

It was as my sister Julie moved away, and I stepped closer to the rail overlooking the sheer drop below, that I sensed something grave and inexplicable come over me. Standing there with Libby clenched against my chest, my body became taut with a deep feeling of dread. Suddenly an intense and almost irresistible urge to throw my precious baby over the side of the rail and into the valley below overwhelmed me. I became frozen while a deep fear grew inside. Unable to move, I had no power over this intensely invasive feeling which held me captive for what seemed an endless time.

This holiday had come up unexpectedly. A few weeks before this, I'd had no idea that I would be spending three weeks with my sister on this 4000-kilometre round trip. Julie and her friend had been planning it for months but, when her friend had to pull out at the last minute, Julie had asked if I'd like to accompany her and share the driving. Everything was already organised: the route plotted and caravan parks booked, so I knew I wouldn't have to worry about any of the details. It was a wonderful opportunity – I loved a good road trip, and I felt very blessed to be asked.

Unusual as it was to do such a long drive with a baby, my husband was very supportive of me going. But while I was excited, I did feel somewhat conflicted about leaving my two young boys behind. Although Steve was a very hands-on father, Tim at five and Michael, three, were quite a handful. However, with his blessing and knowing that my mum was more than willing to help with the kids, I decided to go ahead with it.

This trip had come at a good time. I hadn't been feeling myself for a few months and a couple of friends had suggested I might be experiencing post-natal depression.

I didn't know what was wrong, I loved being a mum and as well as being an answer to prayer, Libby was such an easy-going baby compared to how my boys had been. But there seemed to be an emptiness developing in me, like nothing mattered. I was managing very well with the three children, but it was as if I couldn't feel anything, just a deep sadness.

Leaving Adelaide, we had a tent and all the trappings needed to stay in caravan parks on the way. The plan was to stay with a friend of Julie's for several days, then drive on a few hours further and visit with our younger sister who had moved to Queensland to train as a midwife.

Looking back, it was a big undertaking, but Julie and I got along well and Libby, being such a mellow baby, slept most of the time. The trip itself turned out to be straightforward and pleasant, but whatever it was that I was going through in myself seemed to drain me and everything felt so arduous. While I loved the driving and the adventure of doing this incredible trip, it felt like a part of me was dead inside; I was just doing what I had to do, while my feelings had somehow shrivelled up. Every part of me was on autopilot. I had thought this trip might help but it almost seemed as if being away from the busyness of caring for my whole family and having more time for myself was bringing it all to the surface. I didn't know anything about depression and had been fine after my boys' births, but this was weighing on me more and more.

The possibility, however, of my having post-natal depression was difficult to understand because of the remarkable significance of how my daughter came to be born. She was literally an answer to prayer. Steve and I had two lovely boys, but I had known deep in myself that our family was not complete. There simply had to be another child for us. Being of a tomboyish nature and not at all into girly things, it wasn't about particularly wanting a daughter. I loved having sons. It was just that I absolutely knew that our family was not finished.

There was one major hitch, and that was my husband's agreeance. He was very happy with two children. He loved his boys and being a good provider and protector, he felt that was enough for us. No matter how much I pleaded, tried to convince with logic or used my feminine wiles, he would not budge. It was when he began to talk of permanent measures that, in deep desperation, I did what I probably should have done at the beginning and that was to pray. I let go of my nagging and pressure on Steve and started holding onto God for an answer.

Not long after this, one night at our home-group meeting Steve had been asked to choose and read a passage from the Bible that had significance for him. He chose Hannah's prayer in the book of Samuel where she is thanking God for his provision on the birth of her child when it had seemed an impossibility. It was a scripture that had meaning for him through a past personal situation and nothing at all to do with actual children.

As I heard him reading, however, God shot an arrow of faith into my heart. It was a solid, real, strong faith and I instantly believed with no doubt at all that we would have another child. I did not know when; God didn't give me that insight and I had to come to terms with the fact that it might be many years away. However, along with the word from God in my heart, I experienced an absolute peace and reassurance, and I knew with no reservation that it would happen. I prepared myself for a long wait. But six months later when we were out with friends I was completely caught by surprise when Steve turned to me and said he thought we should have another child.

That child was Libby, so I know she is meant to be here, very definitely. And yet it was while on this trip away that Satan, the master destroyer, tried to take that precious gift that God had given us. That day at the lookout, I almost succumbed to the evil forces that seemed to have me physically frozen while feeling so compelled to throw my gift from God over the edge.

Although that disturbing experience probably only lasted for a few minutes, it felt like hours. Suddenly, not even knowing why or how, something impelled me to take a step back. Immediately, I was then able to turn and stride away.

Feeling very shaken, but not able to share what had happened with my sister, we left the look-out. Resuming our driving, Julie took the wheel and turned the music up as I gazed out the window. It took me several hours to regain my composure. From there the rest of our trip continued smoothly and ended well, but the memory of that confounding and potentially destructive experience stayed with me.

I'd never experienced anything like that before, and thankfully never did again. But while it shook me deeply, it did signify the worst of what I came to recognise as post-natal depression and from that point on it slowly improved.

If you are concerned that you, or someone you know, may be struggling with postnatal anxiety or depression, please call PANDA (Perinatal Anxiety and Depression Australia) on 1300 726 306 (9am-7:30pm AEST) or visit their website (www.panda.org.au) for information.

Teenage Hangout
Leah Grant

On cold winter nights, we dashed from the car parked on the street. Racing to beat my siblings, I would bound over the bluestone gutter filled with wet leaves, heading towards the keypad. The driveway was long and wide with a carport that had to be left vacant for ambulance access. The code was changed regularly and the door clicked when entry was permitted. It didn't matter how often the number combination was updated, I always knew it off by heart.

    I was unapologetically aware of the noise whirlwind we created in the silent corridor, expansive lounge area, followed by more wide walkways. In all other parts of my life, I lacked confidence as a fifteen-year-old but here my inhibitions diminished. Here, under this roof, I belonged. This was my stomping ground. My shoulders automatically straightened and I ran without hesitation. My footsteps were silenced by the carpet (that wasn't really carpet but the type of flooring designed specifically for aggressive cleaning). Another right turn, and I was there seconds before my sisters and brother came through the door. Dad was left behind with his politeness costing him prime position.

    Arriving first meant dibs on the green armchair. It was by far the most comfortable option despite the plastic feel; it was positioned near the bay window. The TV view was unobstructed by the bed in the centre of the room. Most importantly, it was the closest seat to my Mum's delicate hand. There was nowhere in the world I would rather be than in her company. She was my mountain of perspective. Time spent in this room was a gift.

    Over the years of almost daily visits, I became comfortable with the unpredictability of her mood, responses, or if she would be awake. It didn't disappoint me when she was silent and only looked at me with her kind blue eyes. She might not even nod or appear to be listening at all. On those days, I still had hope. Hope that she was understanding and wanted to hear my stories. It was uncommon, but a welcomed surprise when Mum was sitting up in her bed, smiling and ready to engage. Her short brown hair freshly combed by the nurses, and barely creased by her pillow that she spent most of the day resting on.

I have her smile, it's big and joyous.

This was her room and her most common location. If we visited during the day, she might be in her chair by the roses in the lounge. Residents thirty to forty years older than her would be sitting close by. They had reached the end of a long life and now their minds or bodies had slowed.

This is where I came dressed in white before my debutante ball in Year 10. The nurses fussed over me with insistent compliments, trying to make up for the sadness they saw in the scene in front of them. Their empathy brushed off me; aware but choosing not to acknowledge, I smiled at the camera. They saw a heart-breaking situation, a family being eroded by illness. They looked at my youth and saw the grief that lay ahead of me. I pushed forward without imagining the doctor's predictions. I leaned on my faith and prayed for a miracle. I did whatever I could to make her smile, and checked she was warm and comfortable.

I was 16 and 11 months when we faced the inevitable loss and funeral. Days after her passing, we climbed into the car for one last trip. Everything looked the same. I couldn't help but move at my usual speed and enter her room first. I knew the bed would be empty; I had prepared myself for that. I was curious about how that would feel. But I was totally unprepared for what I saw. All her belongings were gone. A different TV was in the corner. I saw a photo frame of a family that wasn't ours. The green chair was in its usual position. The bed had the same white sheets and blankets but it wasn't empty. I could see the shape of feet and I froze.

I had come to say goodbye to this space, to sort and pack her belongings. My haste had given the nurses no chance to warn me. Mum's property had already been packed into boxes and placed in the family waiting room, at the front of the nursing home. I edged away from the room. I didn't belong here anymore. My family didn't belong here anymore. The code would change and we wouldn't be sent the update.

From the outside, our story was heartbreakingly sad. For me, her time in care was filled with memories of bonding with my family. I remember how we set off the fire alarm with her birthday cake, resulting in a special visit from the fire brigade. She smiled and laughed that day. It was such a fuss and such a funny one. We played tennis with balloons, watched musicals endlessly, and just sat in silence sometimes. We read to her, updated her, prayed with her, and kissed her. I've now lived longer without her than with her. I'll never stop learning from her strength and forever I'll keep saying goodbye. The older I get the more I see her smile in the mirror.

It's taken me seventeen years to realise how much I needed to revisit this room, so I write to remember and say goodbye to a place that was an uncommon teenager hangout.

It's Really a Miracle

Jenny Woolsey

April 2004

'Oh my goodness, I can feel her brain pulsating!' I exclaimed. 'The lump's getting bigger! Come here and feel this, Joe.'

My husband placed his fingers on top of our daughter Melissa's head, frowned and nodded.

'That's not good.'

'I'm calling the hospital,' I said, butterflies flapping and swirling around my stomach. 'They have to investigate it now.'

This lump had appeared in 2002 on our three-year-old's skull and the doctors were watching it. Now it was suddenly growing and we were terrified.

Melissa was born in 2001 with a rare craniofacial syndrome called Crouzon syndrome. It was passed on to her from me, her mother. One symptom is the premature fusion of the skull sutures (soft spots) – Craniosynostosis. At nine months of age, Melissa underwent her first surgery to expand the back of her skull to release the pressure being exerted on her brain from the fusion. A second surgery, at eighteen months, expanded and moved her forehead forward.

Both surgeries were harrowing to journey. The lump appeared after the second surgery and it seemed to us that her brain was pushing its way out of her head – and we were worried!

My call to the hospital led to the plastic surgeon referring Melissa to the neurosurgeon. A CT scan showed that our fears were correct. The dura, which is the membrane enveloping the brain, was pushing up between two adjoining skull bones. Surgery was necessary to fix it.

As we waited for the date, the lump continued to grow and enquiries to the hospital led nowhere, which was frustrating and upsetting. We worried that Melissa might fall over and bump the spot and, if she did, could she get brain damage?

May…June…nothing…July…nothing. And the lump continued to grow and pulsate.

September fast approached and, after the school holidays, I would be returning to the primary school classroom from eight months' maternity leave. Our baby, Nicholas, who was born that year in February, also with Crouzon syndrome, needed his first skull expansion so I had asked the plastic surgeon and neurosurgeon if both surgeries could be done before I went back to school. The dates finally arrived. Nicholas was scheduled for November and Melissa in the first week of the December school holidays. Not what I had asked for.

In November, Nicholas's frontal skull expansion surgery went smoothly and the doctors were happy. A couple of days later, though, he developed a fever. As this was abnormal, meningitis was suspected and he was immediately isolated under quarantine conditions.

Skull reconstructions cause the eyes to swell and close and, not being able to see, Nicholas began to mix up night and day. This would have been okay except that my anxious husband would fall asleep on the parent bed, leaving me to entertain Melissa. The poor sleeps, no support from friends and my mental health deterioration took their toll. I was an emotional and physical mess.

Joe did not want to stay overnight to give me a night off so it was suggested by the doctors that I spend a few hours away from the hospital, and they would look after the children if Joe fell asleep. Leaving the hospital walls was wonderful. The sunshine was warm and browsing the markets cleared my head. I was thrilled to also find a Thomas the Tank Engine blanket to take back to Nicholas.

Nicholas progressed and was discharged a week later than originally planned. School expected me back in two days. Joe pressed the lift down button and we waited to go home. I was drained and desperate to get out of there.

'Stop. Don't go,' a female voice called from behind us. 'The doctor wants to ask you something.'

A nurse stood there. 'Why?' was all I could mutter and my heart leaped. This wasn't normal. We turned and backtracked to the ward.

The neurosurgeon's registrar soon appeared. 'There's been a cancellation for tomorrow and we want to do Melissa.'

'Oh,' I said, my mind swirling. This was not good for me. I had already taken more time off work for Nicholas than planned. I knew my class's parents wouldn't like my continued absence after I'd just returned, nor would my boss. I also knew that Melissa needed this surgery ASAP and if the doctors wanted to do it tomorrow then I should just say 'yes' without any hesitation. But it wasn't that easy. My brain zig-zagged back and forth. Work – my daughter – work – my daughter…

The doctor waited for my response.

'Fine,' I said, frowning. *My daughter needed this surgery and all things happened for a reason.* 'Do it.'

I took a deep breath and shuddered. I dreaded having to ring my principal.

We were shown to a bed for Melissa and the nurse found some pyjamas for her. Joe took Nick home. He would come back the next day with Melissa's bag.

From midnight, Melissa fasted and was then rolled down on her bed into the green theatre waiting room. A mask was placed over her small nose and mouth and she drifted off. I kissed her and left, sucking back my tears.

The next step was phoning my boss. I prayed he would be understanding. My gut twisted and I felt nauseous.

After a brief explanation to him, the response came, 'You what?'

'I won't be coming back for the rest of the year. She's in theatre now having neurosurgery.'

'I have parents already complaining and wanting to know why you came back when you've already left again! I have no more teacher relief money so I'll have to split up your class and that's on you!' the principal said.

I hung up and dissolved into tears. Huge sobs whacked my body as I leaned against the wall for support. My heart was punctured with work guilt and my boss's tirade.

'He's soooo mean!' I spluttered. 'He is sooooooo mean.' My husband tried to calm me down but I was distraught.

The long surgery wait lay ahead and I pushed school from my mind.

After six hours, we again saw our little cherub in the paediatric intensive care unit. The neurosurgeon arrived at the bed.

'It wasn't what I expected. There were tears in the dura and I had to push her brain back down into her skull. I then had to take a lining from her thigh muscle to repair the dura.' He ran his hand through his hair and stared into my scared eyes. 'Now, the area of the brain I pushed is the right side of her body, so' – he paused – 'she most likely won't be able to walk again.'

I gasped. 'Oh God, no, please!' I cried. Tears burst from my eyes as I stared at my little angel with her golden hair, asleep on the crisp white sheets, with too many tubes attached and monitors blinking and beeping. Her head was bandaged and her eyes were swelling shut. The nurse standing to the side gave me a sympathetic smile.

The neurosurgeon left and I hugged Joe.

During the night, I tossed and turned on the parent stretcher. My darling girl. She didn't deserve this.

I prayed. *Oh God, it isn't fair. Please may she walk!* My faith wasn't as strong at that point as it had been a decade before, and we weren't attending a church, but I knew God would be listening.

The next day, the neurosurgeon arrived. His lips set. My heart raced. 'Okay, let's see,' he said. I nodded.

He placed his hand on the sole of Melissa's right foot. 'Melissa,' he said, 'can you push my hand with your right foot?'

I held my breath and watched for any movement. I couldn't see any. I looked at the neurosurgeon's face. His lips were still set.

He moved his hand to Melissa's left foot. 'Can you push my hand with your left foot?'

I watched her foot. Again, I couldn't tell. I searched his face.

'That's a good girl, Melissa.'

Icicles sprinted up and down my spine as I waited for his verdict. I prayed. *Please God, may there be movement!* I didn't dare speak.

The neurosurgeon looked at me and said, 'I'll get the physio to come and see her. She will be able to walk.' He then shook his head. 'It's really a miracle.'

More tears welled in my eyes and I heard God whispering to me, 'It's going to be okay. I am in control.'

Insight from a Blacksmith
Craig Chapman

Air surges up through the forge as the blower takes effect. Flames leap as the small, carefully constructed fire roars to life. A crackling sound emerges as I begin to add fuel in the form of chunks of coke. Gravel crunches beneath my feet as I step back between applications to avoid the worst of the eye-stinging, bituminous fumes caused by the fuel's dusty residue. It quickly burns away and the pure, intense heat of a coke fire becomes established. Rain patters lightly on the roof of my open-sided workshop. I am in a good place.

Meg, my ever-alert border collie, sprawls in her usual spot on the path outside the workshop. She will occasionally wander in to inspect progress and receive some affection.

I switch my gaze to the rusty strip of metal on the bench, anticipating the satisfaction of turning a piece of scrap into an object of beauty and function.

The battery-powered blower is the only concession to modern technology in this place. Everything else is indicative of a process which has remained largely unchanged for centuries, even millennia. I feel connected to an ancient wisdom.

The fire is now hot enough. I position the rusty piece of steel in the forge. Soon it is glowing bright orange. I take it out and begin hammering it on the anvil; the first of many cycles. Back in the forge it goes as the heat dissipates. Heat…hammer…heat…hammer… Gradually, the object takes shape. I revel in the creativity, the capacity to form something unique.

I think of the master craftsman, fashioning me according to his will. I too, have been through the fire many times, emerging stronger, more resilient, better equipped to fulfil my purpose. No wonder there are so many Bible references to being refined by fire. It can seem like torture at the time. We have to focus on the end product.

Eventually, the forging is finished. My creation is ready for grinding, cleaning and painting. Most of the imperfections will be removed or disguised. Those which remain will help to tell the story of this piece, adding to its character.

I leave the workshop, pleased with what I have made and at peace with my place in the world.

Is it Enough?

Val Russell

'Hey hun! Look at this!' I held the newspaper up for him to read the headlines: 'Eight dead as bombers target Western-owned Jakarta hotel'.

'The Marriott? We were there at that very table only two weeks ago!' Eyes wide, he grabbed the paper. 'That is so weird. That could have been us!' Just one of many near misses for our family.

'Yes. How many times is that now?' I looked at him.

No response. His mind was elsewhere, his eyes staring into the distant abyss of memory, trying to comprehend the incidents. Years before, he had been standing in a cafe in Bali looking for a missing student. That cafe was bombed hours after he left. It's hard to imagine how different life would be today had he been a victim of the bombing.

God protected our family, not just once but several times. We knew that he loved us and cared for us, though sometimes we have taken that for granted.

Twelve years later, my husband, who fought many a spiritual battle and dodged bombs in foreign countries through the guidance of our Lord, now lives with Early Onset Alzheimer's Disease. A different type of bomb, one that shatters the brain, making it irrational, dysfunctional. One that cripples and destroys the familiarity of life and changes the future forever.

This is our life. This is my life.

Maybe I have needed what has blown my way to become a better human being. Has it worked? Am I a better person?

I first noticed something was amiss a few years ago. I thought it a bit odd that the measurements my husband was trying to make were incorrect. Who was I to correct him? He was a tech guy. He didn't make mistakes measuring wood, well, not that I had ever seen in our thirty-three years of marriage. That year I watched him take a lot longer to complete the projects he engaged in. Sad to say, it still requires enormous effort and time to complete tasks that were once as simple as buttering bread.

It is so challenging watching my perfectionist husband struggle with the simplest of tasks. His self-worth has been terribly crushed, as my beautiful man, with a high IQ, fights to comprehend new information. He has retained, though, an amazing ability to tell fascinating, captivating stories from long ago.

What I admire most is his ability to make light of the situation; even when I see his frustration and hopelessness, he cracks a joke. His jokes either leave me bent double in laughter, or pulling at my hair in frustration because it was simply not funny! I have learned to live with both. The way I react has been very important, if not vital, to the future of our relationship. Sometimes the lion rages inside me, occasionally sneaking past the layer of patience and tolerance I usually wear.

I have had to learn to do new things, manage issues and documents I was only slightly aware existed. Whilst I rose to the challenge, it was not easy. There has been resistance from my husband as he had to relinquish some of the control to me. He eventually realised the energy it took for him to manage everything no longer existed. It made him feel useless. He is not. I couldn't do without him.

Is it Enough?

My husband's memory appears, at times, to be selective and can be twisted with strands of other memories or desires before it emerges. Often, I will stare at him for a few seconds, comprehending. Finding the way to respond is challenging but it's crucial to respond in a positive light. Pointing out the mix up of information causes more anger and frustration for him and that, once again, is not my intention. He will be convinced that he has told me a piece of information when he hasn't, and he will often believe I have agreed with something that I haven't even known about. Once triggered, he will remember the Bali incident and others. He will retell the story with ease, adding extra information to make it sound better.

'Where are my keys?' He is frantic, pacing from room to room looking for them.
    'Where did you last have them?' As soon as the words were out of my mouth, I knew it was a dumb question.
    'If I knew that, I would know where they are!' His frustration was escalating, and I wasn't helping.
    'Take my keys,' I offered, to calm him down. It didn't work. He was determined to find them. Incidents like these can be very traumatic for all involved.

Watching one's soul mate of forty-one years slowly deteriorate is distressing. When I feel overwhelmed, I find myself unable to keep up with the things I love, like my garden, music, writing. Keeping myself motivated and moving is a huge effort and I am not always successful. It is a crippling disease for all involved. One that severely impacts family life, one that is terminal sometime in the future.

Within thirty minutes I have answered the question 'What day is it today?' at least four times. I try to stay calm because I know he cannot help it.

I must consciously try to spend time with my family, but life throws its curve balls which are sometimes difficult to catch. I know when my husband finally succumbs to this horrible, unfair disease, I will miss him terribly. I will feel half of me is missing.

'What have you done with the purple container?' I can never find things when he unloads the dishwasher, but I am thankful he has been helping around the place.

'I have no idea what you are talking about. What purple container? What does it look like?' A typical response, and no matter how clever I am at describing it, he won't be able to recognise it until I show him the container. I cannot show him because I cannot find it.

'Don't worry. I will find it.' I forget not to ask him where things are because he doesn't know he put them away earlier.

'I'm so tired!' he sighs as I arrive home from work. 'I've been working hard today, splitting wood for the fire.' I look at him. He does look tired.

'Have you drunk anything today?' I ask.

'Not that I remember. Oh! I had a coffee at breakfast time.'

Is it Enough?

'You need to eat and drink, mate. I will have to start making you lunch before I go to work.'

'No! You don't need to do that. I eat when I'm hungry and I'm not hungry. I'm capable of making my lunch' is his consistent reply. I know he is, but he doesn't make his food.

I began a discussion about phones. He asked me to wait till he had finished his sudoku game. He needs to concentrate because he is always trying to beat his own time. I waited. I waited some more.

'Are you ready for our discussion now?' My gentle reminder because I knew he had moved onto a different game, totally forgetting I had asked to speak with him.

'Oh, yes, of course! I'm nearly finished this game.' Finally, our discussion begins. It is easy to feel rejected. I tell myself everyday it's the disease speaking.

'How do I see what you are seeing on your phone?' Clearly, he has no idea what to look for, how to find the internet on his phone.

'The button at the bottom with the compass on it.'

'Oh yeah, that's right.' He is annoyed at himself for not being able to remember. There is nothing he can do about it. It is out of his control. This debilitating disease robs my husband of a fulfilling life.

My husband is very caring, full of passion and concern for anyone. He will talk to total strangers with amazing confidence, whereas I am very reserved and hesitant to show how much I care. Maybe we complement each other. It is well-known that opposites attract.

We have clearly seen God's presence and perfect timing in our lives both overseas and in Australia. Our perspective on life has changed. I appreciate the little things more than I did before and feel guilty for some of the big things in life that so many people don't have. However, my current focus must be helping my husband live his life to the fullest it can be as he battles the effects of dementia.

Is it enough?

Maybe what has blown my way has been necessary to develop the skills I didn't have. It is not always just about becoming 'better', but more about understanding the protection God has had over my life, and overcoming the hurdles that have hindered me being who God intended me to be.

I am getting there. Will I ever arrive? Probably not, but I have more strategies and skills than before and that, to me, is an achievement. God has been our rock, our prayer, our lifeline, his nature our inspiration and comfort while living in a physically and spiritually challenging world. I have God on my side, vouching for me all the way, caring and protecting my family, and that...is enough!

The Long Road
Liisa Grace-Baun

My head was throbbing as I struggled to open my eyes. Lying flat on my back with a needle in my arm, I could hear a rhythmic beeping sound beside my bed. The curtains were closed and on the other side people were talking in a serious tone. I tried to move, then suddenly realised I was shackled to the bed. I was in hospital, but what had happened? Please God, help me. Desperately I tried to call out, but I had no voice. Tears were falling down my face and I was unable to wipe them away. Why, oh why, was it so hard for me to stop drinking? This must have been the tenth time that I had landed myself in hospital with alcohol poisoning.

Upon discharge, I always agreed and committed to therapy, whether it be attending Alcoholics Anonymous recovery meetings or sessions with a psychologist. During one of these sessions, I was asked a range of questions to determine whether I had a problem with alcohol. One question was 'How many blackouts have you had? Has it been more than ten throughout your life?' Every part of my being just wanted to lie, I wanted to say less than ten but truth was that I'd had more blackouts than I could count.

As a little girl I had attended social dance nights with my parents at the Finnish hall. It was my job to empty ashtrays into a bucket whilst the adults danced. I liked the way these adults became funny and entertaining once they were intoxicated. Whilst going from table to table, emptying ashtrays, I took sips from glasses on the tables that still had alcohol in them. Initially, I was filled with tremendous fear as I boldly embarked on finishing people's drinks. I knew I shouldn't touch what wasn't mine but the warm sensation that went through my whole body was enough to make me want more. I was only eight years old at the time.

During my teen years I would often go to the creek with my friends. I asked one of the older boys who was of legal age to buy me a bottle of alcohol with the money I handed him. He came back with a bottle of Rosso Antico which I guzzled like it was lemonade! In what seemed like the blink of an eye, I was literally rolling drunk, climbing to the top of the bank and then rolling into the creek over and over again. I felt so free, all my inhibitions disappeared. I suddenly had an instant boost of confidence and courage. This was the first time that I drank to the point of being sick. Later that night, I found myself in the back of a police car being driven home to my father's house. I was twelve years old at the time and little did I know that my compulsion for alcohol had only just begun. Alcohol brought out a very wild side of me. It momentarily removed my inner turmoil. Once that liquor entered my system, I felt no more pain.

In my early twenties I surrendered my life to God. I wanted nothing more than to please him and live a good wholesome life. Raising my children with unconditional love in a Christian home was my goal. I sometimes purchased a cask of wine, drinking it in the evenings for comfort. Alcohol became my companion. Each time I drank, I pleaded with God to forgive me. I managed to go for some length of time without drinking until the compulsion hijacked my sobriety again. I felt on fire for God, reading his word daily and praying for hours at a time. I loved reading scriptures; my children also loved me reading Bible stories to them. I went into ministry as a high school chaplain, taught Sunday school and attended every Bible study that I could.

I would drink secretly, keeping a bottle of wine and glass hidden in my wardrobe. I always knew that I had a problem with alcohol because I didn't drink like others did. If I consumed a couple of wines whilst out with a friend, then I would return home via the bottle shop, polishing off a whole bottle before going to bed.

I withdrew from people when I was drinking. I mostly drank alone and kept it secret from everyone including my children. They would sometimes find my hidden bottles; at times they'd find me passed out with my head in the toilet bowl. The frustration and self-condemnation were overwhelming. Feelings of guilt intensified with each drunken encounter. I would drink more in the hope of numbing all of these negative feelings. I was miserable living a double life. I would minister to others in the church yet I was a drunk behind closed doors.

Falling to my knees, I begged God to help me! I didn't want to drink, yet I could not stop. I cannot count how many times I promised him that I wouldn't drink again. Every excuse or reason to drink was justified in my mind. I drank when I was happy, I drank when I was sad. Whether I was confused, lonely, scared, frustrated or excited. I simply liked to drink.

Both of my biological parents were chronic alcoholics, which is why I was adopted. My father drank himself to death at the age of thirty-four. My mother developed cirrhosis of the liver, dying in her early seventies.

Whenever I looked into my children's eyes, I could see their hurt. They wanted Mum to be sober. I was fun and spontaneous, but they also needed stability.

I went to see pastors and elders, pouring out my struggle. My whole being was engulfed in this vicious cycle. I was swimming in what seemed a never-ending pool of guilt, frustration and shame. The more intoxicated I became, the more guilt, shame and hurt would weave deep into my soul, prompting me to listen to the enemy's deceptive voice, 'You aren't the mother you wanted to be, you were born a reject, no good can come out of your life'.

I was a member of a large church in Adelaide which made it easy to mask my pain. In desperation, I met with a female pastor and shared with her my desire to be free from drinking alcohol. She sat across from me, listening as I shared the battle I was trapped in. I told her how I had been prayed for many times, yet I still kept falling back into my drinking. She prayed for me, passed me the tissue box and told me to hold firm to God's promises and sin no more.

As I walked to my car, my steps felt lighter, my heart was filling with hope again and I truly believed that this time I would not go back to drinking. The following Sunday morning my head felt like it was weighted down with a tonne of bricks; the intensity of the pain was affecting my vision. I had drunk two bottles of wine the night before.

I felt so powerless. I was able to stop drinking for days, weeks, months, sometimes even a couple of years but the obsession never went away. What was I doing wrong? Or what wasn't I doing right?

In 2011, two of my brothers passed away, three months apart, from alcoholism. Needless to say, I was overcome with grief. I wish I could say that's where the drinking all ended but it didn't. It wasn't until years later that I had a revelation that alcoholism was a disease centred in the mind.

That is when God led me to a Christian recovery group called Free-N-One (Free from drugs and alcohol and One in Christ). Enthusiastically I joined the group, which was accessible via Zoom due to the global pandemic. My heart was overjoyed seeing so many other Christians who also battled alcoholism. They shared their experience, strength and hope. Joining this recovery group was like coming home. I suddenly had an extended family.

I still encounter problems and struggles, but I no longer seek to escape them for I am confident in God to share openly in my support group. Alcohol is no longer an option as I have adopted healthy, new strategies for coping with life's adversities as they arise. The inner peace I possess through the strength and hope I have in God sustains me daily.

On the Job

Steph Penny

Things did not turn out the way I planned.

I didn't plan to leave the job I loved. I never planned to walk away from one income without having another lined up. I certainly never planned to wind up unemployed, frantically scouring job websites for new places to call home.

But unplanned circumstances sometimes have a way of bringing something even better into our lives.

I left that job because it had become untenable. I tried everything I could to make it work, but things slowly deteriorated over a period of six months. Finally, it seemed the writing was on the wall. The job was unsalvageable. Here I was, a thoroughly experienced and passionate professional counsellor, unable to stay on the job.

I had been unemployed only once before. It was a desperate situation then too. I trusted God with my life back then as I walked out of my old job, pleading for him to provide. And God did provide another job, just in the nick of time. I had been mere days away from running out of money when a fabulous job materialised out of thin air. They wanted me to start work immediately. *Thank you, God*, I had breathed. No need to move back home with my parents!

So having seen God provide before, not only with that job but with other needs like money, friendship, petrol, and healing, I knew God could create and align circumstances to meet my needs. I knew my life was squarely in God's grip and he would see me through. Somehow.

On the Job

I started looking for a new job before the old job collapsed under me. I had friends in other workplaces who had upcoming positions – gifts of hope from God at a time I sorely needed it. But nothing came of those opportunities. One by one they fell through. I left my old job without any new offers.

Leaving without having the next job lined up was not easy. Unemployment is always a highly undesirable position in which to voluntarily place oneself, and this situation was no exception. I felt disappointed and embarrassed to be without a job after fifteen years in the field.

I had a conversation with God straight away. 'Right. Here we are. Before we do this, I need to decide right here and now whether I am going to trust you completely or not at all. I am not going to start looking for work and then start worrying about it. Either I trust you, or I don't. So right now, I choose to trust you. I will do my bit – looking for work – and entrust the rest to you.'

I am not saying this was the right or wrong thing to do. I did what I felt I needed to do at the time. God had come through for me before and I knew he would not forget or neglect me. God was surely on the job, working behind the scenes to bring things together for my good. Armed with that simple trust, I commenced the tedious and thankless task of job-seeking.

Looking for work was full-time work for me. I was up at six in the morning, working on cover letters for positions, writing job applications well into the evening. Sifting through available positions was time-consuming. There were lots of jobs available but not many that caught my enthusiasm. I didn't just want a job that paid. I wanted a job that would last the distance. I worked diligently and applied for a range of jobs that genuinely sparked my interest. I was rewarded with a few decent job interviews. But none of them seemed to get off the ground.

About three weeks into this stretch of unemployment, I sensed God speaking to me. I had been praying about the whole unemployment situation, trying to surrender to him afresh – not for the first time – when I sensed him say, 'Don't underestimate me.'

'Oh, okay God,' I replied. I assumed I knew what he meant: that he was ultimately in control of my new job. Fine by me. I was happy to keep doing my job-seeking bit and let God do his bit.

But God wasn't finished. 'Don't underestimate me,' he continued, 'because I can do more than you think. I am going to create something for you that you could have never imagined. So keep your eyes peeled.'

I didn't know what to say except for, 'Wow – okay then!' If God wanted to do something creative and new, if vague and unspecified, I was here for it.

A couple of weeks later I was invited to yet another job interview, my ninth so far. It was a frontline role that I thought would be exciting and challenging, and I would be working for a great organisation to boot. I travelled by train to the head office for the interview. When I sat down in the interview room, the panel took one look at me and said, 'What are you doing here? We've seen your resume and you are way overqualified for this role.'

I was a little taken aback. 'Well,' I rallied, 'I actually thought this role would be challenging. Plus, it's a role where I can bring my wealth of clinical experience to bear.' They seemed to accept this explanation. The interview proceeded and it seemed to go well, despite me being a little back-footed. At the end they sat back and looked hard at me.

'We still think you have way too much experience for this role,' they declared. I was not sure what to say. Had I made a mistake in coming? Had I wasted their time – and mine?

Then the unexpected happened. The head interviewer leaned forward eagerly. 'We have some new mental health programs opening up at the moment,' she smiled. 'How would you like to do some work for us in the new programs?'

My face flushed. 'I'd be delighted!' I yelped. Did I sound a little too enthusiastic? They said they would get back to me with a job offer. They said they loved my extensive experience and really wanted to hire me.

They saved the best for last. 'So, Steph, if you could design your ideal job, what would it look like?' I stared at them. My brain was buzzing. I thought, *This is not how job interviews are supposed to go!* I tried to keep calm, and described my perfect job: the role, the conditions, the salary, the location. They nodded and said, 'We'll see what we can do.' With that, the interview was over.

I walked out of the office into the warm afternoon air, my head spinning, my feet barely touching the ground. *This was not supposed to happen*, I thought to myself. *You are supposed to find a job, apply for it, and either you succeed or you don't. You are not supposed to go in for one job and get offered a completely different one tailored to your specifications!*

My heart pounded as I walked, going over the interview in my mind. I pressed the button at the crosswalk and as I stood there waiting, a bell rang in the back of my brain. I recalled God had said something about expecting the unexpected. I suddenly said out loud, 'God, is this what you meant by, "I can do more than you can imagine"?'

I'm not sure he answered. I'm not sure he needed to. I already knew the answer. He had done way more than I had ever expected.

They did come back to me with a job offer, almost exactly to my specifications. They couldn't give me the salary I wanted, being an NGO (Non-Government Organisation), but that was okay because they ticked every other box. Of course, I accepted. And I have been very happy in this new job.

I am grateful that things did not go according to plan after all. Even when I lost my old job, I never needed to worry about employment, not even for a second. God was on the job.

The Wild Elephant that Obeyed the Lord
Wendy Radford

My mother was a church planter by call, and she often went to extremely rural areas in the Darjeeling foothills with church folk, to share Christ's love with the villagers. One Christmas, she took a group of young Sunday School kids and a few teachers for Christmas carolling to the surrounding villages. They travelled in an old mini-van that probably drove no faster than forty kilometres an hour, and was driven by an older man whom we called Baje (grandfather). Of course, for a greater sense of protection, my brother-in-law was roped in to go along with the vanload of women and children.

On their way back, they had to pass through a thick forest which we knew often had wild elephants roaming through it. As the van chugged along, close to dusk, a cyclist tried to wave them down from the side of the road, but they did not stop. Going a bit further, Baje slammed on the brakes, the singing of Christmas carols stopped, and they looked ahead of them. In the centre of the road was a wild elephant, a few metres away. Baje was so taken aback that he switched the van's headlights off and then on again. In his fright, Baje did this a few times, until my mother scolded him to stop.

The flashing headlights infuriated the elephant, and it began to pace, a few steps back and then a few steps forward, a movement they make when getting ready to charge. As the elephant charged, my mother shouted, 'Let us pray' and a roar of prayers, simultaneously prayed, went up to the Lord. My brother-in-law decided he was not going to pray or close his eyes, as he watched the elephant charging, getting a front-row view, sitting next to the driver.

The elephant came charging towards the van, and then stopped just in front of it as the frightened group of women and children shouted 'Amen'! The wild elephant peered in through the front windscreen, looked in, shook its head from side to side, then turned and walked away into the forest.

There was pin-drop-silence as Baje started the van and quickly drove away. The group, upon their return, looked pale but with a story to tell, of how 'even the wild elephants obey the Lord'.

Behind the Wall

Esther Cremona

Once upon a time, I prayed. Fervently, with an open heart and with genuine faith. Normal for me was purposefully making time to chat with the Almighty, around chronic illness, living with a disability, study, work and sole parenting two young children. Praying in the car, in the shower, cooking dinner – or as part of a life group. Sometimes prayer was as short as 'God help me'– especially when I was about to lose either my sanity or my temper, or both. I liked to partake in a simple thanks for the day, voice an impassioned plea for a friend's healing or cast a worry or three the Lord's way. I have raised my glass of shiraz to him and exclaimed, 'Thanks for creating grapes!'

I'm often awed at hearing people speak enthusiastically about their prayer life. 'I get up at 5.30am every morning to spend time with God' they happily exclaim, or 'my whole family sit together every evening and do our devotions. We can't do without them'. I used to understand the delight and eagerness to pray, but at the moment I'm better at ducking and weaving even the notion of praying.

I cannot pinpoint the exact moment the prayers started to slip from my grasp, or when a stone wall started its tenuous assembly to entomb my heart. I do know that I am a fabulous procrastinator. I like to pretend that I'm doing all the things that need to be done and doing them well. I wonder if the finite art of perfecting procrastination and a gradual decrease in deliberate prayer are relatives in disharmony. I believe the two are definitely connected, as uncomfortable as they are with one another. Instead of finding a few minutes to pray, or locating a quiet spot to reflect and consider being thankful, I procrastinate.

The ability to procrastinate is frowned upon by both secular and faith-filled communities.

If there is an art to delaying certain things that need to be done, I am, indubitably, a creative genius. A simple example is cleaning out the fridge. Easy done, right? With my wandering mind and slightly awkward body, the planned task might go something like this:

Open the door to the fridge, remove containers with mildly festering contents.

Remember the kids' uniforms need to be washed.

Leave the fridge, enter the laundry.

Kitty litter looks dire – clean immediately.

Have I fed the cats?

Back in the kitchen, the flower vase needs a refill!

Oh, look at that box of filing that needs to be sorted instantly.

Find a recipe that must be cooked. Look in the kitchen for ingredients.

Note: we have run out of bread.

Drive to the bakery, because we need bread.

Bread going in the spare freezer in the garage.

Take hammer and screwdriver off freezer and put away in storage cupboard...

...the cupboard that contains a box of life memorabilia. Impromptu reminiscing proceeds.

Enter daydreams of my trip to Texas many years ago.

Melancholia invades, feel resentment for my chronic illness preventing overseas trips.

Sigh.

Need a cup of tea and a home-made peanut butter cup.

Read a chapter or two of *Jane Eyre*, watch the last half-hour of the MasterChef catch-up episode.

Odd socks need sorting. While I'm sitting down.

The cat meows for outside time.

I'm up again.

I'll water the plants while I'm outside.

I'll bring the towels in; they are now dried to a hardened shell in the Australian sun.

Hungry kids: *Muuuuum, what's for dinner?*

Open the fridge.

The fridge needs a clean out.

It reads like a comical confusion of internal musings and physical meandering. The kids have clean uniforms and I am content to read – but how the heck did I completely avoid the one task I wanted to accomplish?

Prayers have met the same fate as the fridge. It's just not happening. Prayer, wherefore art thou? Seriously, where did the prayer go? The thing is, I know the answer.

My health has deteriorated consistently, as a result of living with a progressive neuro-muscular illness. Well-intentioned prayers have been spoken over my body, asking God for a miraculous healing, but I am not anyone's miracle to boast about.

I am a Christian. I am disabled. I am divorced. I am resolutely unashamed to be Christian, disabled and divorced. Although, some days I check that I'm not wearing a neon sign – or custom-printed t-shirt – that says: 'Please attach stigma here'.

When I faced a brand-new health challenge, resulting in surgery in 2021, foundations were laid for the wall of separation between myself and a heartfelt prayer. I began to refute the idea that as a Christian I must always find joy in my challenges. I rebutted any hint to find delight through days of excruciating pain and blocked out uninvited and impractical advice. Sometimes, driving the kids to school is the highlight of my day, or the only time I spend outside of my home.

It's been relatively easy to live as a partial recluse, as I spend many days at home alone, accountable to no-one. Grief is present in daily life, as I pine for being able to undertake the simplest of tasks: hold and carry a cup independently, hang washing up on a clothes line, or open a jar lid. I want to take my kids for walks on the local beach, or a hike up Waterfall Gully. I miss going anywhere without someone always asking, 'What's *wrong* with you?' and looking me up and down, frowning.

I can write lists. To-do lists, noted in moments of sporadic clarity as I am determined to manage the basics of 'adulting'. Still not praying about strength or wisdom or even considering asking God for help; procrastination over prayer. I've become stubborn in building my wall of separation. Every brick that has been piled on is heavy, and I feel the weight on my heart.

I start one task and if it becomes wearisome, I quickly find a distraction. Rather than pray about it or open up further grief by acknowledging the loss of an activity I can no longer do, I meander and find something I can do. Almost everything I manage to do is frustratingly slow and my occasional outburst of expletives could shock delicate ears, yet I persist. Without praying about it. The technical term for my procrastination is that of an 'avoider'.

I've become the mistress of avoidance. The queen of throw-it-all-together-at-the-last-possible-minute. I avoid allowing any trickle of sunlight to pervade the dense wall around my heart. I avoid showing vulnerability. I avoid people. I avoid church. I avoid prayer.

I imagine Jesus sighing and brushing off his robes, before offering his hand to me and proclaiming, 'I rose again, I can help you! Please ask me. Maybe we can have a chat. Seriously, I'd really like to catch up sometime.' Unfailingly polite, I would probably answer, 'Thanks, but no thanks.'

Switching off prayer and switching on procrastination has presented an interesting conundrum as I commenced part-time studies in 2022. A Certificate in Creative Writing and Communication. Writing an assignment for Creative Non-Fiction and the word 'vulnerability' has been bandied about – a lot. I'd mentioned my resistance to prayer during a writing exercise, but without feeling any true conviction.

Procrastination teamed up with 'Imposter Syndrome' to make it even trickier to write with candid frankness. I messed up the due date for my major assessment. I sent a brief message to one of my classmates, bemoaning my *faux pas*. She replied with a prayer for my words to flow.

I wrote, 'Dear Lord – what she said!'

The response? 'Prayer suspension over.'

Mere days later, the women's pastor from my church called 'just to check in.' She prayed for all the right words to be written, and to feel at peace submitting my assignment. She prayed for the softening of my hardening heart. As did a faithful friend that I spoke with later that same week.

I cannot exclaim, 'Hallelujah, I've seen the prayer light' at this moment in time. My prayer life might be on hiatus but I know God's grace and forgiveness are always available. God is patiently chipping away at my resistance, gently and persistently, to let the first slivers of sunshiny light break through the wall.

My Sister Amy

Natalie Ingram

Seven-year-old Amy sat upright in bed as her father read from the first chapter of Ruth.

This Bible story had remained amongst her top-five most-requested bedtime stories for the last year and George wasn't about to discourage Amy from listening to the Bible – despite his having to read Ruth so much that he'd almost committed it to memory.

Amy's dad cleared his throat and continued, 'And Ruth said, "Intreat me not to leave thee, or to return from following after thee: for whither thou goest, I will go; and where thou lodgest, I will lodge: thy people shall be my people, and thy God my God."'

'Wait, Daddy,' Amy interrupted.

George looked up from the page and saw his daughter's creased face. *I've definitely explained what these funny Old English words mean before and she seemed to cope alright with them.*

Amy fixed her gaze on the text between them. She was quiet for a while before explaining her confusion. 'Daddy, I want to be like Ruth…I want your God to be my God.'

George craned his head back and went speechless. His body looked very still but inside a chill of excitement sprang along his spine. *Where on earth did this come from?*

He knew Amy had the tendency to be reflective – even for a child. And he also knew she had a genuine interest in Bible stories. But to find out that she saw her dad had a God which she felt she didn't have, and that she wanted very much to share, shocked and delighted him. *This is what Amy must have noticed in Ruth too: a desire to know God like her mother-in-law, Naomi, did!*

He stopped reading and led his daughter in a prayer to Jesus.

Several nights later, Amy would surprise him again. She knocked on her parents' bedroom door and waited for George to find his way to her in the dark. Stumbling and with eyes twitching from the hallway light, he asked, 'What is it? Are you alright?'

'Daddy, how many times do I need to ask Jesus to forgive me and to come into my life?'

George, though sleepy, nearly cried! 'Once Amy…just once,' he croaked quietly. 'Jesus forgives you for all time and he will always stay with you.'

This introspective young girl turned seventeen.

Sometime during the year, the whole family – which consisted of George, his wife and their five children – went to Stradbroke Island to play at the beach with their cousins. It was a proper summer's day, perfect for swimming! George's wife stayed mostly undercover, caring for their youngest children and George enjoyed cricket with the older ones. They shared their guardian duties with Amy's aunts and uncles who'd joined in on the holiday.

Tom, one of the older cousins, was a fit, twenty-something year-old and he'd found a good place to swim. He'd been out there for some time and Amy longed to join him.

She was an experienced swimmer and she loved all things water. In truth, whenever the Christmas holidays rolled around, she spent many long days playing in the family's inflatable swimming pool or going to the beach with George. Even as a teenager, she continued to live up to her reputation as the family's best 'water baby'.

Her curiosity and desire to swim at this new beach finally got the better of her, and she began making her way out to Tom.

I might as well see if I can get to where he is; I'm sure he's not that far!

She swam out towards him bit by bit, metre by metre, spurred on by the refreshing waves and the sight of her cousin in the closing distance. As she went further though, she found herself beginning to tire quicker than expected; she couldn't explain it but the waves felt like they were getting stronger somehow.

This isn't right! It's not usually like this! I can't seem to go where I want to and I'm being pulled around…and down…

Amy's mind began to panic as she felt the waves growing more powerful by the second, pushing her deeper and deeper into their control. She couldn't hold them off. It was too much. Her body was moving fast out to sea and there was no-one around to bring her back to shore.

She'd lost sight of the sand, lost sight of her family and lost any confidence she'd had with swimming. She felt utterly helpless.

Help me! Someone! she wailed.

'Lord, I need two things,' she prayed. 'If I die, please, somehow, keep Mum and Dad from finding out!'

Then, after a gush of water sloshed heavily against the side of her face, she prayed again. 'And also, if I do have to die, I'm okay with that as I know I'll go to be with you…But I would also rather live, if that's okay!'

In that moment, whether God audibly spoke it or not, she wasn't sure, but she felt she just had to look to her right. As she turned her head in that direction she saw, out of nowhere, two complete strangers having a lark metres away from her.

With this revelation, she mustered the strength to wave her hands as wildly as she could, desperate to catch their attention. But her efforts were short-lived as the blustering waves overpowered so much of her movement that she became exhausted.

As she continued struggling to keep her head above the water, one of the guys suddenly caught her eye contact and motioned, *Are you alright?*

She tried to speak but no sound came out. So instead, she attempted to once more flail her arms about hoping they'd understand she was saying, *No! I'm really not alright, I need help!*

Apparently, her message was received loud and clear! In what felt like seconds, the young men were by her side each taking one of Amy's arms and driving her body out of the rip.

'It's okay. Breathe!' the older of them instructed. When Amy had obeyed he repeated himself, 'Take a breath. You're okay. Take another breath.'

Bit by bit, the trio made their way to shore. All Amy could do was listen to her rescuers' instructions and obey. It was the longest two-minute swim she'd ever experienced!

She thanked them – probably sixteen or seventeen times – as they neared the sand and then insisted on thanking them again as soon as she was out of the water. The guys chuckled as a mixture of relief and pride spread across their faces. When they saw that Amy was alright they gave each other an emphatic high-five before charging straight back into the sea. Amy marvelled at their courage to go immediately back to a place which she knew very nearly claimed her life.

She stood stunned for a few minutes, as the hot afternoon breeze enveloped her, gently removing both the chill and terror from her body. She began to notice the many families dotting the shoreline around her. Some people were playing cricket and others were busy creating sand sculptures. Everyone was in their own world. Everyone was oblivious to what she'd just gone through.

Auntie Mable was the first relative to see Amy walking away from the water. 'Where've you been?' she asked more pointedly than she knew.

The only response she got, though, was a slightly dishevelled, 'I'm alright,' as Amy made her way to the sun shelter. Her mum was there, playing with the baby and completely unaware of what had just happened. Amy silently thanked God for not letting her mum worry and then grabbed her towel.

Over the next hour or so, Amy gradually found the nerve to tell her parents about what she'd just experienced.

Neither of them responded very much after hearing Amy's story but instead busied themselves with packing up and getting all the family together – explaining to their relatives that it was time to go. Amy thought their nonchalant reaction was a little strange but didn't question the decision to leave, for even this 'water baby' had had enough of the sea for one day.

That night, however, Amy tiptoed into the dining room after bedtime, planning to turn the kitchen light off as it had been apparently forgotten. But instead she found George sitting at the table with his Bible out in front of him. He glanced at her warmly so she came up to him and leant against his shoulder to see what he was reading. It was the beginning of Ruth. When Amy saw it she whispered, 'I don't know what I'd do if I didn't have your God, Dad.' Her mind then gave way to the day's events and she squeezed her eyes shut to stop herself from weeping.

George held her tightly. 'Nor me, my darling. I'm so, so grateful that your God is my God too.'

Isn't it time you told your story?

This year, 41 people have had their stories published, and seven of them have been recognised as category winners. Do you have a story of faith and testimony? Will 2023 be the year you tell your story?

For the possibility of being published or winning a prize, please send us your true stories in one of these categories:

Open Category
maximum 1500 words
Short Category
maximum 500 words

Submission details, rules and writing resources can be found on our website:

https://storiesoflife.net

Have you written a book?
Not sure how to get it published?
Worried it will cost a fortune?

Not a problem.

Helping writers to become authors

info@immortalise.com.au
www.immortalise.com.au